G000070358

SELECTED HISTORIC CREEDS, CATECHISMS AND CONFESSIONS:

From the Apostles Creed to The Theological Declaration of Barmen

© 2011 Benediction Classics.

Contents

Apostles' Creed

I believe in God the Father, Almighty, Maker of heaven and earth
And in Jesus Christ, his only begotten Son, our Lord
Who was conceived by the Holy Ghost, born of the Virgin Mary
Suffered under Pontius Pilate; was crucified, dead and buried; He descended into hell.
The third day he rose again from the dead
He ascended into heaven, and sits at the right hand of God the Father Almighty
From thence he shall come to judge the quick and the dead
I believe in the Holy Ghost
I believe a holy catholic church; the communion of saints
The forgiveness of sins
The resurrection of the body
And the life everlasting. Amen.

Nicene Creed 325 AD

I believe in one God, the Father Almighty, Maker of heaven and earth, and of all things visible and invisible.

And in one Lord Jesus Christ, the only-begotten Son of God, begotten of the Father before all worlds; God of God, Light of Light, very God of very God; begotten, not made, being of one substance with the Father, by whom all things were made.

Who, for us men for our salvation, came down from heaven, and was incarnate by the Holy Spirit of the virgin Mary, and was made man; and was crucified also for us under Pontius Pilate; He suffered and was buried; and the third day He rose again, according to the Scriptures; and ascended into heaven, and sits on the right hand of the Father; and He shall come again, with glory, to judge the quick and the dead; whose kingdom shall have no end.

And I believe in the Holy Ghost, the Lord and Giver of Life; who proceeds from the Father and the Son; who with the Father and the Son together is worshipped and glorified; who spoke by the prophets.

And I believe one holy catholic and apostolic Church. I acknowledge one baptism for the remission of sins; and I look for the resurrection of the dead, and the life of the world to come. Amen.

Athanasian Creed

Whosoever will be saved, before all things it is necessary that he hold the catholic faith; Which faith except every one do keep whole and undefiled, without doubt he shall perish everlastingly.

And the catholic faith is this: That we worship one God in Trinity, and Trinity in Unity; Neither confounding the persons nor dividing the substance. For there is one person of the Father, another of the Son, and another of the Holy Spirit.

But the Godhead of the Father, of the Son, and of the Holy Spirit is all one, the glory equal, the majesty coeternal. Such as the Father is, such is the Son, and such is the Holy Spirit. The Father uncreated, the Son uncreated, and the Holy Spirit uncreated. The Father incomprehensible, the Son incomprehensible, and the Holy Spirit incomprehensible. The Father eternal, the Son eternal, and the Holy Spirit eternal. And yet they are not three eternals but one eternal. As also there are not three untreated nor three incomprehensible, but one untreated and one incomprehensible. So likewise the Father is almighty, the Son almighty, and the Holy Spirit almighty. And yet they are not three almighties, but one almighty. So the Father is God, the Son is God, and the Holy Spirit is God; And yet they are not three Gods, but one God. So likewise the Father is Lord, the Son Lord, and the Holy Spirit Lord; And yet they are not three Lords but one Lord. For like as we are compelled by the Christian verity to acknowledge every Person by himself to be God and Lord; So are we forbidden by the catholic religion to say; There are three Gods or three Lords. The Father is made of none, neither created nor begotten. The Son is of the Father alone; not made nor created, but begotten. The Holy Spirit is of the Father and of the Son; neither made, nor created, nor begotten, but proceeding. So there is one Father, not three Fathers; one Son, not three Sons; one Holy Spirit, not three Holy Spirits. And in this Trinity none is afore or after another; none is greater or less than another. But the whole three persons are coeternal, and coequal. So that in all things, as aforesaid, the Unity in Trinity and the Trinity in Unity is to be worshipped. He therefore that will be saved must thus think of the Trinity.

Furthermore it is necessary to everlasting salvation that he also believe rightly the incarnation of our Lord Jesus Christ. For the right faith is that we believe and confess that our Lord Jesus Christ, the Son of God, is God and man. God of the substance of the Father, begotten before the worlds; and man of substance of His mother, born in the world. Perfect God and perfect man, of a reasonable soul and human flesh subsisting. Equal to the Father as touching His Godhead, and inferior to the Father as touching His manhood. Who, although He is God and man, yet He is not two, but one Christ. One, not by conversion of the Godhead into flesh, but by taking of that manhood into God. One altogether, not by confusion of substance, but by unity of person. For as the reasonable soul and flesh is one man, so God and man is one Christ; Who suffered for our salvation, descended into hell, rose again the third day from the dead; He ascended into heaven, He sits on the right hand of the Father, God, Almighty; From thence He shall come to judge the quick and the dead. At whose coming all men shall rise again with their bodies; and shall give account of their own works. And they that have done good shall go into life everlasting and they that have done evil into everlasting fire.

This is the catholic faith, which except a man believe faithfully he cannot be saved.

The Heidelberg Catechism

Introduction

Lord's Day 1

Question 1

What is thy only comfort in life and death?

That I with body and soul, both in life and death, [5] am not my own, [6] but belong unto my faithful Saviour Jesus Christ; [7] who, with his precious blood, has fully satisfied for all my sins, [8] and delivered me from all the power of the devil; [9] and so preserves me [10] that without the will of my heavenly Father, not a hair can fall from my head; [11] yea, that all things must be subservient to my salvation, [12] and therefore, by his Holy Spirit, He also assures me of eternal life, [13] and makes me sincerely willing and ready, henceforth, to live unto him. [14]

[5] Rom. 14:7, 8.
[6] 1 Cor. 6:19.
[7] 1 Cor. 3:23; Tit. 2:14.
[8] 1 Pet. 1:18, 19; 1 John 1:7; 1 John 2:2, 12.
[9] Heb. 2:14; 1 John 3:8; John 8:34-36.
[10] John 6:39; John 10:28; 2 Thess. 3:3; 1 Pet. 1:5.
[11] Matt. 10:29-31; Luke 21:18.
[12] Rom. 8:28.
[13] 2 Cor. 1:20-22; 2 Cor. 5:5; Eph. 1:13, 14; Rom. 8:16.

[14] Rom. 8:14; 1 John 3:3.

Question 2

How many things are necessary for thee to know, that thou, enjoying this comfort, mayest live and die happily?

Three; [15] the first, how great my sins and miseries are; [16] the second, how I may be delivered from all my sins and miseries; [17] the third, how I shall express my gratitude to God for such deliverance. [18]

[15] Matt. 11:28-30; Luke 24:46-48; 1 Cor. 6:11; Tit. 3:3-7.
[16] John 9:41; John 15:22.
[17] John 17:3; Acts 4:12; Acts 10:43 .
[18] Eph. 5:8-11; 1 Pet. 2:9, 10; Rom. 6:1, 2, 12, 13.

The First Part--Of The Misery Of Man

Lord's Day 2

Question 3

Whence knowest thou thy misery?

Out of the law of God. [19]

[19] Rom. 3:20.

Question 4

What does the law of God require of us?

Christ teaches us that briefly, Matt. 22:37-40, "Thou shalt love the Lord thy God with all thy heart, with all thy soul, and with all thy mind, and with all thy strength. This is the first and the great commandment; and the second is like unto it, Thou shalt love thy neighbour as thyself. On these two commandments hang all the law and the prophets." [20]

[20] Deut. 6:5; Lev. 19:18; Mark 12:30 ; Luke 10:27.

Question 5

Canst thou keep all these things perfectly?

In no wise; [21] for I am prone by nature to hate God and my neighbour. [22]

[21] Rom. 3:10, 20, 23; 1 John 1:8, 10.
[22] Rom. 8:7; Eph. 2:3; Tit. 3:3; Gen. 6:5; Gen. 8:21; Jer. 17:9; Rom. 7:23.

Question 6

Did God then create man so wicked and perverse?

By no means; but God created man good, [23] and after his own image, [24] in true righteousness and holiness, that he might rightly know God his Creator, heartily love him and live with him in eternal happiness to glorify and praise him. [25]

[23] Gen. 1:31.
[24] Gen. 1:26, 27.
[25] Col. 3:9, 10; Eph. 4:23, 24; 2 Cor. 3:18.

Lord's Day 3

Question 7

Whence then proceeds this depravity of human nature?

From the fall and disobedience of our first parents, Adam and Eve, in Paradise; [26] hence our nature is become so corrupt, that we are all conceived and born in sin. [27]

[26] Gen. 3; Rom. 5:12, 18, 19.
[27] Ps. 51:5; Gen. 5:3.

Question 8

Are we then so corrupt that we are wholly incapable of doing any good, and inclined to all wickedness?

Indeed we are; [28] except we are regenerated by the Spirit of God. [29]

[28] Gen. 8:21; John 3:6; Gen. 6:5; Job 14:4; Job 15:14, 16, 35; Isa. 53:6.
[29] John 3:3, 5; 1 Cor. 12:3; 2 Cor. 3:5.

Lord's Day 4

Question 9

Does not God then do injustice to man, by requiring from him in his law, that which he cannot perform?

Not at all; [30] for God made man capable of performing it; but man, by the instigation of the devil, [31] and his own wilful disobedience, [32] deprived himself and all his posterity of those divine gifts.

[30] Eph. 4:24; Eccl. 7:29.

[31] John 8:44; 2 Cor. 11:3; Gen. 3:4 .
[32] Gen. 3:6; Rom. 5:12; Gen. 3:13; 1 Tim. 2:13, 14.

Question 10

Will God suffer such disobedience and rebellion to go unpunished?

By no means; but is terribly displeased [33] with our original as well as actual sins; and will punish them in his just judgment temporally and eternally, [34] as he has declared, "Cursed is every one that continueth not in all things, which are written in the book of the law, to do them."
[35]

[33] Gen. 2:17; Rom. 5:12.
[34] Ps. 5:5; Ps. 50:21; Nah. 1:2; Exod. 20:5; Exod. 34:7; Rom. 1:18; Eph. 5:6; Heb. 9:27.
[35] Deut. 27:26; Gal. 3:10.

Question 11

Is not God then also merciful?

God is indeed merciful, [36] but also just; [37] therefore his justice requires, that sin which is committed against the most high majesty of God, be also punished with extreme, that is, with everlasting punishment of body and soul.

[36] Exod. 34:6, 7; Exod. 20:6.
[37] Ps. 7:9; Exod. 20:5; Exod. 23:7; Exod. 34:7; Ps. 5:5, 6; Nah. 1:2, 3
.

The Second Part--Of Man's Deliverance

Lord's Day 5

13

Question 12

Since then, by the righteous judgment of God, we deserve temporal and eternal punishment, is there no way by which we may escape that punishment, and be again received into favour?

God will have his justice satisfied: [38] and therefore we must make this full satisfaction, either by ourselves, or by another. [39]

[38] Gen. 2:17; Exod. 20:5; Exod. 23:7; Ezek. 18:4; Matt. 5:26; 2 Thess. 1:6; Luke 16:2.
[39] Rom. 8:3, 4.

Question 13

Can we ourselves then make this satisfaction?

By no means; but on the contrary we daily increase our debt. [40]

[40] . Job 9:2, 3; Job 15:15, 16; Job 4:18, 19; Ps. 130:3; Matt. 6:12; Matt. 18:25; Matt. 16:26.

Question 14

Can there be found anywhere, one, who is a mere creature, able to satisfy for us?

None; for, first, God will not punish any other creature for the sin which man has committed; [41] and further, no mere creature can sustain the burden of God's eternal wrath against sin, so as to deliver others from it. [42]

[41] Ezek. 18:4; Gen. 3:17; Heb. 2:14-17.
[42] Nah. 1:6; Ps. 130:3.

Question 15

What sort of a mediator and deliverer then must we seek for?

For one who is very man, and perfectly [43] righteous; [44] and yet more powerful than all creatures; that is, one who is also very God. [45]

[43] 1 Cor. 15:21; Jer. 33:16; Isa. 53:9; 2 Cor. 5:21.
[44] Heb. 7:16, 26.
[45] Isa. 7:14; Isa. 9:6; Rom. 9:5; Jer. 23:5, 6 ; Jer. 23:6; Luke 11:22.

Lord's Day 6

Question 16

Why must he be very man, and also perfectly righteous?

Because the justice of God requires that the same human nature which has sinned, should likewise make satisfaction for sin; [46] and one, who is himself a sinner, cannot satisfy for others. [47]

[46] Ezek. 18:4, 20; Rom. 5:12, 15, 18; 1 Cor. 15:21; Heb. 2:14-16; 1 Pet. 3:18; Isa. 53:3-5, 10, 11.

[47] Heb. 7:26, 27; Ps. 49:7, 8; 1 Pet. 3:18.

Question 17

Why must he in one person be also very God?

That he might, by the power of his Godhead [48] sustain in his human nature, [49] the burden of God's wrath; [50] and might obtain for, and restore to us, righteousness and life. [51]

[48] Isa. 9:6; Isa. 63:3.
[49] Isa. 53:4, 11.
[50] Deut. 4:24; Nah. 1:6; Ps. 130:3.
[51] Isa. 53:5, 11; Acts 2:24; 1 Pet. 3:18; John 3:16; Acts 20:28; John 1:4.

Question 18

Who then is that Mediator, who is in one person both very God, [52] and a real [53] righteous man? [54]

Our Lord Jesus Christ: [55] "who of God is made unto us wisdom, and righteousness, and sanctification, and redemption." [56]

[52] 1 John 5:20; Rom. 9:5; Rom. 8:3; Gal. 4:4; Isa. 9:6; Jer. 23:6; Mal. 3:1.
[53] Luke 1:42; Luke 2:6, 7; Rom. 1:3; Rom. 9:5; Philip. 2:7; Heb. 2:14, 16, 17; Heb. 4:15.
[54] Isa. 53:9, 11; Jer. 23:5; Luke 1:35; John 8:46; Heb. 4:15; Heb. 7:26; 1 Pet. 1:19; 1 Pet. 2:22; 1 Pet. 3:18.
[55] 1 Tim. 2:5; Heb. 2:9; Matt. 1:23; 1 Tim. 3:16; Luke 2:11.
[56] 1 Cor. 1:30.

Question 19

Whence knowest thou this?

From the holy gospel, which God himself first revealed in Paradise; [57] and afterwards published by the patriarchs [58] and prophets, [59] and represented by the sacrifices and other ceremonies of the law; [60] and lastly, has fulfilled it by his only begotten Son. [61]

[57] Gen. 3:15.
[58] Gen. 22:18; Gen. 12:3; Gen. 49:10, 11.

[59] Isa. 53; Isa. 42:1-4; Isa. 43:25 ; Isa. 49:5, 6, 22, 23; Jer. 23:5, 6; Jer. 31:32, 33; Jer. 32:39-41; Mic. 7:18-20; Acts 10:43; Rom. 1:2; Heb. 1:1; Acts 3:22-24; Acts 10:43; John 5:46.
[60] Heb. 10:1, 7; Col. 2:7; John 5:46.
[61] Rom. 10:4; Gal. 4:4, 5; Gal. 3:24; Col. 2:17.

Lord's Day 7

Question 20

Are all men then, as they perished in Adam, saved by Christ?

No; [62] only those who are ingrafted into him, and, receive all his benefits, by a true faith. [63]

[62] Matt. 7:14; Matt. 22:14.
[63] Mark 16:16; John 1:12; John 3:16, 18, 36; Isa. 53:11; Ps. 2:12; Rom. 11:17, 19, 20; Rom. 3:22; Heb. 4:2, 3; Heb. 5:9 ; Heb. 10:39; Heb. 11:6.

Question 21

What is true faith?

True faith is not only a certain knowledge, whereby I hold for truth all that God has revealed to us in his word, [64] but also an assured confidence, [65] which the Holy Ghost [66] works by the gospel in my heart; [67] that not only to others, but to me also, remission of sin, everlasting righteousness and salvation, [68] are freely given by God, merely of grace, only for the sake of Christ's merits. [69]

[64] James 2:19.
[65] 2 Cor. 4:13; Eph. 2:7-9; Eph. 3:12; Gal. 2:16; Heb. 11:1, 7-10; Heb. 4:16; James 1:6; Matt. 16:17; Philip. 1:19; Rom. 4:16-21; Rom. 5:1; Rom. 1:16; Rom. 10:10, 17; Rom. 3 :24.25.

[66] Gal. 5:22; Matt. 16:17; 2 Cor. 4:13; John 6:29; Eph. 2:8; Philip. 1:19; Acts 16:14.

[67] Rom. 1:16; Rom. 10:17; 1 Cor. 1:21; Acts 10:44; Acts 16:14.

[68] Rom. 1:17; Gal. 3:11; Heb. 10:10 , 38; Gal. 2:16.

[69] Eph. 2:8; Rom. 3:24; Rom. 5:19; Luke 1:77, 78.

Question 22

What is then necessary for a christian to believe?

All things promised us in the gospel, [70] which the articles of our catholic undoubted christian faith briefly teach us.

[70] John 20:31; Matt. 28:19; Mark 1:15 .

Question 23

What are these articles?

1. I believe in God the Father, Almighty, Maker of heaven and earth: 2. And in Jesus Christ, his only begotten Son, our Lord: 3. Who was conceived by the Holy Ghost, born of the Virgin Mary: 4. Suffered under Pontius Pilate; was crucified, dead, and buried: He descended into hell: 5. The third day he rose again from the dead: 6. He ascended into heaven, and sitteth at the right hand of God the Father Almighty: 7. From thence he shall come to judge the quick and the dead: 8. I believe in the Holy Ghost: 9. I believe a holy catholic church: the communion of saints: 10. The forgiveness of sins: 11. The resurrection of the body: 12. And the life everlasting.

Lord's Day 8

Question 24

How are these articles divided?

18

Into three parts; the first is of God the Father, and our creation; the second of God the Son, and our redemption; the third of God the Holy Ghost, and our sanctification.

Question 25

Since there is but one only divine essence, [71] why speakest thou of Father, Son, and Holy Ghost?

Because God has so revealed himself in his word, [72] that these three distinct persons are the one only true and eternal God.

[71] Deut. 6:4; Eph. 4:6; Isa. 44:6; Isa. 45:5; 1 Cor. 8:4, 6.
[72] Isa. 61:1; Luke 4:18; Gen. 1:2, 3; Ps. 33:6; Isa. 48:16; Ps. 110:1; Matt. 3:16, 17; Matt. 28:19; 1 John 5:7; Isa. 6:1, 3; John 14:26; John 15:26; 2 Cor. 13:13; Gal. 4:6; Eph. 2:18; Tit. 3:5, 6 .

Lord's Day 9

Question 26

What believest thou when thou sayest, "I believe in God the Father, Almighty, Maker of heaven and earth"?

That the eternal Father of our Lord Jesus Christ (who of nothing made heaven and earth, with all that is in them; [73] who likewise upholds and governs the same by his eternal counsel and providence) [74] is for the sake of Christ his Son, my God and my Father; [75] on whom I rely so entirely, that I have no doubt, but he will provide me with all things necessary for soul and body [76] and further, that he will make whatever evils he sends upon me, in this valley of tears turn out to my advantage; [77] for he is able to do it, being Almighty God, [78] and willing, being a faithful Father. [79]

[73] Gen. 1, 2; Job 33:4; Job 38, 39; Ps. 33:6; Acts 4:24; Acts 14:15; Isa. 45:7.
[74] Matt. 10:29; Heb. 1:3; Ps. 104:27-30; Ps. 115:3; Matt. 10:29; Eph. 1:11.
[75] John 1:12; Rom. 8:15; Gal. 4:5-7; Eph. 1:5.
[76] Ps. 55:23; Matt. 6:25, 26; Luke 12:22.
[77] Rom. 8:28.
[78] Rom. 10:12; Luke 12:22; Rom. 8:23; Isa. 46:4; Rom. 10:12.
[79] Matt. 6:25-34; Matt. 7:9-11.

Lord's Day 10

Question 27

What dost thou mean by the providence of God?

The almighty and everywhere present power of God; [80] whereby, as it were by his hand, he upholds and governs [81] heaven, earth, and all creatures; so that herbs and grass, rain and drought, [82] fruitful and barren years, meat and drink, health and sickness, [83] riches and poverty, [84] yea, and all things come, not by chance, but be his fatherly hand. [85]

[80] Acts 17:25-28; Jer. 23:23, 24; Isa. 29:15, 16; Ezek. 8:12.
[81] Heb. 1:3.
[82] Jer. 5:24; Acts 14:17.
[83] John 9:3.
[84] Prov. 22:2.
[85] Matt. 10:20; Prov. 16:33.

Question 28

What advantage is it to us to know that God has created, and by his providence does still uphold all things?

That we may be patient in adversity; [86] thankful in prosperity; [87] and that in all things, which may hereafter befall us, we place our firm trust in our faithful God and Father, [88] that nothing shall separate us from his love; [89] since all creatures are so in his hand, that without his will they cannot so much as move. [90]

[86] Rom. 5:3; James 1:3; Ps. 39:9; Job 1:21, 22.
[87] Deut. 8:10; 1 Thess. 5:18.
[88] Ps. 55:22; Rom. 5:4.
[89] Rom. 8:38, 39.
[90] Job 1:12; Job 2:6; Acts 17:25, 28; Prov. 21:1.

Lord's Day 11

Question 29

Why is the Son of God called "Jesus", that is a Saviour?

Because he saveth us, and delivereth us from our sins; [91] and like-wise, because we ought not to seek, neither can find salvation in any other. [92]

[91] Matt. 1:21; Heb. 7:24, 25.
[92] Acts 4:12; John 15:4, 5; 1 Tim. 2:5; Isa. 43:11; 1 John 5:11.

Question 30

Do such then believe in Jesus the only Saviour, who seek their salva-tion and welfare of saints, of themselves, or anywhere else?

They do not; for though they boast of him in words, yet in deeds they deny Jesus the only deliverer and Saviour; [93] for one of these two things must be true, that either Jesus is not a complete Saviour; or that they, who by a true faith receive this Saviour, must find all things in him necessary to their salvation. [94]

21

[93] 1 Cor. 1:13, 30, 31; Gal. 5:4.
[94] Heb. 12:2; Isa. 9:6; Col. 1:19, 20; Col. 2:10; 1 John 1:7, 16.

Lord's Day 12

Question 31

Why is he called "Christ", that is anointed?

Because he is ordained of God the Father, and anointed with the Holy Ghost, [95] to be our chief Prophet and Teacher, [96] who has fully revealed to us the secret counsel and will of God concerning our redemption; [97] and to be our only High Priest, [98] who by the one sacrifice of his body, has redeemed us, [99] and makes continual intercession with the Father for us; [100] and also to be our eternal King, who governs us by his word and Spirit, and who defends and preserves us in that salvation, he has purchased for us. [101]

[95] Heb. 1:9; Ps. 45:8; Isa. 61:1; Luke 4:18.
[96] Deut. 18:15; Acts 3:22; Acts 7:37; Isa. 55:4.
[97] John 1:18; John 15:15.
[98] Ps. 110:4.
[99] Heb. 10:12, 14; Heb. 9:12, 14, 28.
[100] Rom. 8:34; Heb. 9:24; 1 John 2:1; Rom. 5:9, 10.
[101] Ps. 2:6; Zech. 9:9; Matt. 21:5; Luke 1:33; Matt. 28:18; John 10:28; Rev. 12:10, 11.

Question 32

But why art thou called a Christian? [102]

Because I am a member of Christ by faith, [103] and thus am partaker of his anointing; [104] that so I may confess his name, [105] and present myself a living sacrifice of thankfulness to him: [106] and also that with a free and good conscience I may fight against sin and Satan in this life [107] and afterwards I reign with him eternally, over all creatures. [108]

[102] Acts 11:26.
[103] 1 Cor. 6:15.
[104] 1 John 2:27; Acts 2:17.
[105] Matt. 10:32; Rom. 10:10; Mark 8:38 .
[106] Rom. 12:1; 1 Pet. 2:5, 9; Rev. 5:8, 10; Rev. 1:6.
[107] 1 Pet. 2:11; Rom. 6:12, 13; Gal. 5:16, 17; Eph. 6:11; 1 Tim. 1:18, 19.
[108] 2 Tim. 2:12; Matt. 24:34.

Lord's Day 13

Question 33

Why is Christ called the "only begotten Son" of God, since we are also the children of God?

Because Christ alone is the eternal and natural Son of God; [109] but we are children adopted of God, by grace, for his sake. [110]

[109] John 1:1-3, 14, 18; Heb. 1:1, 2; John 3:16; 1 John 4:9; Rom. 8:32.
[110] Rom. 8:15-17; John 1:12; Gal. 4:6; Eph. 1:5, 6.

Question 34

Wherefore callest thou him "our Lord"?

Because he hath redeemed us, both soul and body, from all our sins, not with silver or gold, but with his precious blood, and has delivered us from all the power of the devil; and thus has made us his own property. [111]

[111] 1 Pet. 1:18, 19; 1 Pet. 2:9; 1 Cor. 6:20; 1 Cor. 7:23; 1 Tim. 2:6 ; John 20:28.

Lord's Day 14

Question 35

What is the meaning of these words "He was conceived by the Holy Ghost, born of the virgin Mary"?

That God's eternal Son, who is, and continues [112] true and eternal God, [113] took upon him the very nature of man, of the flesh and blood of the virgin Mary, [114] by the operation of the Holy Ghost; [115] that he might also be the true seed of David, [116] like unto his brethren in all things, [117] sin excepted. [118]

[112] Rom. 1:4; Rom. 9:5.
[113] 1 John 5:20; John 1:1; John 17:3; Rom. 1:3; Col. 1:15.
[114] Gal. 4:4; Luke 1:31, 42, 43.
[115] John 1:14; Matt. 1:18, 20; Luke 1:32, 35.
[116] Ps. 132:11; Rom. 1:3; 2 Sam. 7:12; Acts 2:30.
[117] Philip. 2:7; Heb. 2:14, 17.
[118] Heb. 4:15.

Question 36

What profit dost thou receive by Christ's holy conception and nativity?

That he is our Mediator; [119] and with His innocence and perfect holiness, covers in the sight of God, my sins, wherein I was conceived and brought forth. [120]

[119] Heb. 7:26, 27; Heb. 2:17.
[120] 1 Pet. 1:18, 19; 1 Pet. 3:18; 1 Cor. 1:30, 31; Rom. 8:3, 4; Isa. 53:11; Ps. 32:1.

Lord's Day 15

Question 37

What dost thou understand by the words, "He suffered"?

24

That he, all the time that he lived on earth, but especially at the end of his life, sustained in body and soul, the wrath of God against the sins of all mankind: [121] that so by his passion, as the only propitiatory sacrifice, [122] he might redeem our body and soul from everlasting damnation, [123] and obtain for us the favour of God, righteousness and eternal life. [124]

[121] Isa. 53:4; 1 Pet. 2:24; 1 Pet. 3:18; 1 Tim. 2:6.
[122] Isa. 53:10, 12; Eph. 5:2; 1 Cor. 5:7; 1 John 2:2; 1 John 4:10; Rom. 3:25; Heb. 9:28; Heb. 10:14.
[123] Gal. 3:13; Col. 1:13; Heb. 9:12; 1 Pet. 1:18, 19.
[124] Rom. 3:25; 2 Cor. 5:21; John 3:16; John 6:51; Heb. 9:15; Heb. 10:19.

Question 38

Why did he suffer "under Pontius Pilate, as judge"?

That he, being innocent, and yet condemned by a temporal judge, [125] might thereby free us from the severe judgement of God to which we were exposed. [126]

[125] John 18:38; Matt. 27:24; Acts 4:27 , 28; Luke 23:14, 15; John 19:4.
[126] Ps. 69:4; Isa. 53:4, 5; 2 Cor. 5:21; Gal. 3:13.

Question 39

Is there anything more in his being "crucified", than if he had died some other death?

Yes there is; for thereby I am assured, that he took on him the curse which lay upon me; [127] for the death of the cross was accursed of God. [128]

[127] Gal. 3:13.
[128] Deut. 21:23.

Lord's Day 16

Question 40

Why was it necessary for Christ to humble himself even "unto death"?

Because with respect to the justice and truth of God, [129] satisfaction for our sins could be made no otherwise, than by the death of the Son of God. [130]

[129] Gen. 2:17.
[130] Rom. 8:3, 4; Heb. 2:9, 14, 15 .

Question 41

Why was he also "buried"?

Thereby to prove that he was really dead. [131]

[131] Matt. 27:59, 60; Luke 23:52, 53; John 19:38-42; Acts 13:29.

Question 42

Since then Christ died for us, why must we also die?

Our death is not a satisfaction for our sins, [132] but only an abolishing of sin, and a passage into eternal life. [133]

[132] Mark 8:37; Ps. 49:7.
[133] John 5:24; Philip. 1:23; Rom. 7:24 .

Question 43

What further benefit do we receive from the sacrifice and death of Christ on the cross?

That by virtue thereof, our old man is crucified, dead and buried with him; [134] that so the corrupt inclinations of the flesh may no more reign in us; [135] but that we may offer ourselves unto him a sacrifice of thanksgiving. [136]

[134] Rom. 6:6.
[135] Rom. 6:6-8, 11, 12; Col. 2:12.
[136] Rom. 12:1.

Question 44

Why is there added, "he descended into hell"?

That in my greatest temptations, I may be assured, and wholly comfort myself in this, that my Lord Jesus Christ, by his inexpressible anguish, pains, terrors, and hellish agonies, in which he was plunged during all his sufferings, [137] but especially on the cross, has delivered me from the anguish and torments of hell. [138]

[137] Ps. 18:5, 6; Ps. 116:3; Matt. 26:38; Heb. 5:7; Isa. 53:10; Matt. 27:46.
[138] Isa. 53:5.

Lord's Day 17

Question 45

What does the "resurrection" of Christ profit us?

First, by his resurrection he has overcome death, that he might make us partakers of that righteousness which he had purchased for us by his death; [139] secondly, we are also by his power raised up to a new life; [140] and lastly, the resurrection of Christ is a sure pledge of our blessed resurrection. [141]

[139] 1 Cor. 15:16; Rom. 4:25; 1 Pet. 1:3 .
[140] Rom. 6:4; Col. 3:1, 3; Eph. 2:5, 6 .
[141] 1 Cor. 15:12, 20, 21; Rom. 8:11.

Lord's Day 18

Question 46

How dost thou understand these words, "he ascended into heaven"?

That Christ, in sight of his disciples, was taken up from earth into heaven; [142] and that he continues there for our interest, [143] until he comes again to judge the quick and the dead.[144]

[142] Acts 1:9; Matt. 26:64; Mark 16:19; Luke 24:51.
[143] Heb. 7:25; Heb. 4:14; Heb. 9:24; Rom. 8:34; Eph. 4:10; Col. 3:1.
[144] Acts 1:11; Matt. 24:30.

Question 47

Is not Christ then with us even to the end of the world, as he has promised? [145]

Christ is very man and very God; with respect to his human nature, he is no more on earth; [146] but with respect to his Godhead, majesty, grace and spirit, he is at no time absent from us. [147]

[145] Matt. 28:20.
[146] Heb. 8:4; Matt. 26:11; John 16:28; John 17:11; Acts 3:21.
[147] John 14:17-19; John 16:13; Matt. 28:20; Eph. 4:8, 12.

Question 48

But if his human nature is not present, wherever his Godhead is, are not then these two natures in Christ separated from one another?

Not as all, for since the Godhead is illimitable and omnipresent, [148] it must necessarily follow that the same is beyond the limits of the human nature he assumed, [149] and yet is nevertheless in this human nature, and remains personally united to it.

[148] Acts 7:49; Jer. 23:24.
[149] Col. 2:9; John 3:13; John 11:15; Matt. 28:6.

Question 49

Of what advantage to us is Christ's ascension into heaven?

First, that he is our advocate in the presence of his Father in heaven; [150] secondly, that we have our flesh in heaven as a sure pledge that he, as the head, will also take up to himself, us, his members; [151] thirdly, that he sends us his Spirit as an earnest, [152] by whose power we "seek the things which are above, where Christ sitteth on the right hand of God, and not things on earth." [153]

[150] 1 John 2:1; Rom. 8:34.
[151] John 14:2; John 17:24; John 20:17 ; Eph. 2:6.
[152] John 14:16, 7; Acts 2:1-4, 33; 2 Cor. 1:22; 2 Cor. 5:5.
[153] Col. 3:1; Philip. 3:14.

Lord's Day 19

Question 50

Why is it added, "and sitteth at the right hand of God"?

Because Christ is ascended into heaven for this end, that he might appear as head of his church, [154] by whom the Father governs all things. [155]

[154] Eph. 1:20, 21, 23; Col. 1:18.
[155] Matt. 28:18; John 5:22.

Question 51

What profit is this glory of Christ, our head, unto us?

First, that by his Holy Spirit he pours out heavenly graces upon us his members; [156] and then that by his power he defends and preserves us against all enemies. [157]

[156] Acts 2:33; Eph. 4:8.
[157] Ps. 2:9; Ps. 110:1, 2; John 10:28; Eph. 4:8.

Question 52

What comfort is it to thee that "Christ shall come again to judge the quick and the dead"?

That in all my sorrows and persecutions, with uplifted head I look for the very same person, who before offered himself for my sake, to the tribunal of God, and has removed all curse from me, to come as judge from heaven: [158] who shall cast all his and my enemies into everlasting condemnation, [159] but shall translate me with all his chosen ones to himself, into heavenly joys and glory. [160]

[158] Luke 21:28; Rom. 8:23; Philip. 3:20 ; Tit. 2:13; 1 Thess. 4:16.
[159] 2 Thess. 1:6, 8-10; Matt. 25:41-43.
[160] Matt. 25:34; 2 Thess. 1:7.

Lord's Day 20

Question 53

What dost thou believe concerning the Holy Ghost?

First, that he is true and coeternal God with the Father and the Son; [161] secondly, that he is also given me, [162] to make me by a true faith, partaker of Christ and all his benefits, [163] that he may comfort me [164] and abide with me for ever. [165]

[161] 1 John 5:7; Gen. 1:2; Isa. 48:16; 1 Cor. 3:16; 1 Cor. 6:19; Acts 5:3, 4.

[162] Gal. 4:6; Matt. 28:19, 20; 2 Cor. 1:21, 22; Eph. 1:13.
[163] Gal. 3:14; 1 Pet. 1:2; 1 Cor. 6:17 .
[164] Acts 9:31; John 15:26.
[165] John 14:16; 1 Pet. 4:14.

Lord's Day 21

Question 54

What believest thou concerning the "holy catholic church" of Christ?

That the Son of God [166] from the beginning to the end of the world, [167] gathers, defends, and preserves [168] to himself by his Spirit and word, [169] out of the whole human race, [170] a church chosen to everlasting life, [171] agreeing in true faith; [172] and that I am and forever shall remain, [173] a living member thereof. [174]

[166] Eph. 5:26; John 10:11; Acts 20:28 ; Eph. 4:11-13.
[167] Ps. 71:17, 18; Isa. 59:21; 1 Cor. 11:26.
[168] Matt. 16:18; John 10:28-30; Ps. 129:1-5.
[169] Isa. 59:21; Rom. 1:16; Rom. 10:14-17; Eph. 5:26 .
[170] Gen. 26:4; Rev. 5:9.
[171] Rom. 8:29, 30; Eph. 1:10-13.
[172] Acts 2:46; Eph. 4:3-6.
[173] Ps. 23:6; 1 Cor. 1:8, 9; John 10:28; 1 John 2:19; 1 Pet. 1:5.
[174] 1 John 3:14, 19-21; 2 Cor. 13:5; Rom. 8:10.

Question 55

What do you understand by "the communion of saints"?

First, that all and every one, who believes, being members of Christ, are in common, partakers of him, and of all his riches and gifts; [175] secondly, that every one must know it to be his duty, readily and cheerfully to employ his gifts, for the advantage and salvation of other members. [176]

[175] 1 John 1:3; 1 Cor. 1:9; Rom. 8:32; 1 Cor. 12:12, 13; 1 Cor. 6:17.
[176] 1 Cor. 12:21; 1 Cor. 13:1, 5; Philip. 2:4-8.

Question 56

What believest thou concerning "the forgiveness of sins"?

That God, for the sake of Christ's satisfaction, will no more remember my sins, neither my corrupt nature, against which I have to struggle all my life long; [177] but will graciously impute to me the righteousness of Christ, [178] that I may never be condemned before the tribunal of God. [179]

[177] 1 John 2:2; 1 John 1:7; 2 Cor. 5:19 , 21.
[178] Jer. 31:34; Ps. 103:3, 4; Ps. 103:10, 12; Mic. 7:19, 23-25.
[179] Rom. 8:1-4; John 3:18; John 5:24.

Lord's Day 22

Question 57

What comfort does the "resurrection of the body" afford thee?

That not only my soul after this life shall be immediately taken up to Christ its head; [180] but also, that this my body, being raised by the power of Christ, shall be reunited with my soul, and made like unto the glorious body of Christ. [181]

[180] Luke 16:22; Luke 23:43; Philip. 1:21, 23.
[181] 1 Cor. 15:53, 54; Job 19:25, 26; 1 John 3:2; Philip. 3:21.

Question 58

What comfort takest thou from the article of "life everlasting"?

That since I now feel in my heart the beginning of eternal joy, [182] after this life, I shall inherit perfect salvation, which "eye has not seen, nor ear heard, neither has it entered into the heart of man" to conceive, and that to praise God therein for ever. [183]

[182] 2 Cor. 5:2, 3.
[183] 1 Cor. 2:9; John 17:3.

Lord's Day 23

Question 59

But what does it profit thee now that thou believest all this?

That I am righteous in Christ, before God, and an heir of eternal life.
[184]

[184] Hab. 2:4; Rom. 1:17; John 3:36.

Question 60

How are thou righteous before God?

Only by a true faith in Jesus Christ; [185] so that, though my conscience accuse me, that I have grossly transgressed all the commandments of God, and kept none of them, [186] and am still inclined to all evil; [187] notwithstanding, God, without any merit of mine, [188] but only of mere grace, [189] grants and imputes to me, [190] the perfect satisfaction, [191] righteousness and holiness of Christ; [192] even so, as if I never had had, nor committed any sin: yea, as if I had fully accomplished all that obedience which Christ has accomplished for me; [193] inasmuch as I embrace such benefit with a believing heart. [194]

[185] Rom. 3:21-25, 28; Rom. 5:1 , 2; Gal. 2:16; Eph. 2:8, 9; Philip. 3:9.
[186] Rom. 3:9.
[187] Rom. 7:23.
[188] Tit. 3:5; Deut. 9:6; Ezek. 36:22.
[189] Rom. 3:24; Eph. 2:8.
[190] Rom. 4:4, 5; 2 Cor. 5:19.
[191] 1 John 2:2.
[192] 1 John 2:1.
[193] 2 Cor. 5:21.
[194] Rom. 3:22; John 3:18.

Question 61

Why sayest thou, that thou art righteous by faith only?

Not that I am acceptable to God, on account of the worthiness of my
faith; but because only the satisfaction, righteousness, and holiness of
Christ, is my righteousness before God; [195] and that I cannot receive
and apply the same to myself any other way than by faith only. [196]

[195] 1 Cor. 1:30; 1 Cor. 2:2.
[196] 1 John 5:10.

Lord's Day 24

Question 62

But why cannot our good works be the whole, or part of our righteousness before God?

Because, that the righteousness, which can be approved of before the
tribunal of God, must be absolutely perfect, [197] and in all respects
conformable to the divine law; and also, that our best works in this life
are all imperfect and defiled with sin. [198]

[197] Gal. 3:10; Deut. 27:26.
[198] Isa. 64:6.

Question 63

What! do not our good works merit, which yet God will reward in this and in a future life?

This reward is not of merit, but of grace. [199]

[199] Luke 17:10.

Question 64

But does not this doctrine make men careless and profane?

By no means: for it is impossible that those, who are implanted into Christ by a true faith, should not bring forth fruits of thankfulness.[200]

[200] Matt. 7:18; John 15:5.

Lord's Day 25

Question 65

Since then we are made partakers of Christ and all his benefits by faith only, whence does this faith proceed?

From the Holy Ghost, [201] who works faith in our hearts by the preaching of the gospel, and confirms it by the use of the sacraments. [202]

[201] Eph. 2:8, 9; Eph. 6:23; John 3:5; Philip. 1:29.
[202] Matt. 28:19, 20; 1 Pet. 1:22, 23.

Question 66

What are the sacraments?

The sacraments are holy visible signs and seals, appointed of God for this end, that by the use thereof, he may the more fully declare and seal to us the promise of the gospel, viz., that he grants us freely the remission of sin, and life eternal, for the sake of that one sacrifice of Christ, accomplished on the cross. [203]

[203] Gen. 17:11; Rom. 4:11; Deut. 30:6; Lev. 6:25; Heb. 9:7-9, 24; Ezek. 20:12; Isa. 6:6, 7; Isa. 54:9.

Question 67

Are both word and sacraments, then, ordained and appointed for this end, that they may direct our faith to the sacrifice of Jesus Christ on the cross, as the only ground of our salvation? [204]

Yes, indeed: for the Holy Ghost teaches us in the gospel, and assures us by the sacraments, that the whole of our salvation depends upon that one sacrifice of Christ which he offered for us on the cross.

[204] Rom. 6:3; Gal. 3:27.

Question 68

How many sacraments has Christ instituted in the new covenant, or testament?

Two: namely, holy baptism, and the holy supper.

Lord's Day 26

Question 69

36

How art thou admonished and assured by holy baptism, that the one sacrifice of Christ upon the cross is of real advantage to thee?

Thus: That Christ appointed this external washing with water, [205] adding thereto this promise, [206] that I am as certainly washed by his blood and Spirit from all the pollution of my soul, that is, from all my sins, [207] as I am washed externally with water, by which the filthiness of the body is commonly washed away.

[205] Matt. 28:19.
[206] Matt. 28:19; Acts 2:38; Matt. 3:11; Mark 16:16; John 1:33; Rom. 6:3, 4.
[207] 1 Pet. 3:21; Mark 1:4; Luke 3:3

Question 70

What is it to be washed with the blood and Spirit of Christ?

It is to receive of God the remission of sins, freely, for the sake of Christ's blood, which he shed for us by his sacrifice upon the cross; [208] and also to be renewed by the Holy Ghost, and sanctified to be members of Christ, that so we may more and more die unto sin, and lead holy and unblamable lives. [209]

[208] Heb. 12:24; 1 Pet. 1:2; Rev. 1:5; Rev. 7:14; Zech. 13:1; Ezek. 36:25.
[209] John 1:33; John 3:5; 1 Cor. 6:11; 1 Cor. 12:13; Rom. 6:4; Col. 2:12.

Question 71

Where has Christ promised us, that he will as certainly wash us by his blood and Spirit, as we are washed with the water of baptism?

In the institution of baptism, which is thus expressed: "Go ye, therefore, and teach all nations, baptizing them in the name of the Father, and of the Son, and of the Holy Ghost", Matt. 28:19. And "he that believeth, and is baptized, shall be saved; but he that believeth not, shall be damned.", Mark 16:16. This promise is also repeated, where the scripture calls baptism "the washing of regenerations" and the washing away of sins. Tit. 3:5, Acts 22:16. [210]

[210] Tit. 3:5; Acts 22:16.

Lord's Day 27

Question 72

Is then the external baptism with water the washing away of sin itself?

Not at all: [211] for the blood of Jesus Christ only, and the Holy Ghost cleanse us from all sin. [212]

[211] Matt. 3:11; 1 Pet. 3:21; Eph. 5:26 , 27.
[212] 1 John 1:7; 1 Cor. 6:11.

Question 73

Why then does the Holy Ghost call baptism "the washing of regeneration," and "the washing away of sins"?

God speaks thus not without great cause, to-wit, not only thereby to teach us, that as the filth of the body is purged away by water, so our sins are removed by the blood and Spirit of Jesus Christ; [213] but especially that by this divine pledge and sign he may assure us, that we are spiritually cleansed from our sins as really, as we are externally washed with water. [214]

[213] Rev. 1:5; Rev. 7:14; 1 Cor. 6:11 .
[214] Mark 16:16; Gal. 3:27.

Question 74

Are infants also to be baptized?

Yes: for since they, as well as the adult, are included in the covenant and church of God; [215] and since redemption from sin [216] by the blood of Christ, and the Holy Ghost, the author of faith, is promised to them no less than to the adult; [217] they must therefore by baptism, as a sign of the covenant, be also admitted into the christian church; and be distinguished from the children of unbelievers [218] as was done in the old covenant or testament by circumcision, [219] instead of which baptism is instituted [220] in the new covenant.

[215] Gen. 17:7.
[216] Matt. 19:14.
[217] Luke 1:15; Ps. 22:10; Isa. 44:1-3; Acts 2:39.
[218] Acts 10:47.
[219] Gen. 17:14.
[220] Col. 2:11-13.

Lord's Day 28

Question 75

How art thou admonished and assured in the Lord's Supper, that thou art a partaker of that one sacrifice of Christ, accomplished on the cross, and of all his benefits?

Thus: That Christ has commanded me and all believers, to eat of this broken bread, and to drink of this cup, in remembrance of him, adding these promises: [221] first, that his body was offered and broken on the cross for me, and his blood shed for me, as certainly as I see with my eyes, the bread of the Lord broken for me, and the cup communicated to me; and further, that he feeds and nourishes my soul to everlasting life, with his crucified body and shed blood, as assuredly as I receive from the hands of the minister, and taste with my mouth the bread and cup of the Lord, as certain signs of the body and blood of Christ.

[221] Matt. 26:26-28; Mark 14:22-24; Luke 22:19, 20; 1 Cor. 10:16, 17; 1 Cor. 11:23-25; 1 Cor. 12:13 .

Question 76

What is it then to eat the crucified body, and drink the shed blood of Christ?

It is not only to embrace with believing heart all the sufferings and death of Christ and thereby to obtain the pardon of sin, and life eternal; [222] but also, besides that, to become more and more united to his sacred body, [223] by the Holy Ghost, who dwells both in Christ and in us; so that we, though Christ is in heaven [224] and we on earth, are notwithstanding "flesh of his flesh and bone of his bone" [225] and that we live, and are governed forever by one spirit, [226] as members of the same body are by one soul.

[222] John 6:35, 40, 47-54.
[223] John 6:55, 56.
[224] Col. 3:1; Acts 3:21; 1 Cor. 11:26.
[225] Eph. 3:16; Eph. 5:29, 30, 32; 1 Cor. 6:15, 17, 19; 1 John 3:24; 1 John 4:13; John 14:23.
[226] John 6:56-58; John 15:1-6; Eph. 4:15, 16.

Question 77

Where has Christ promised that he will as certainly feed and nourish believers with his body and bleed, as they eat of this broken bread, and drink of this cup?

In the institution of the supper, which is thus expressed: [227] "The Lord Jesus, the same night in which he was betrayed, took bread, and when he had given thanks, he brake it, and: said: eat, this is my body, which is broken for you; this do in remembrance of me. After the same manner also he took the cup, when he had supped, saying: this cup is the new testament in my blood; this do ye, as often as ye drink it, in remembrance of me. For, as often as ye eat this bread, and drink this cup, ye do show the Lord's death till he come." 1 Cor. 11:23-26. This promise is repeated by the holy apostle Paul, where he says "The cup of blessing which we bless, is it not the communion of the blood of Christ? The bread which we break, is it not the communion of the body of Christ? For we being many are one bread, and one body: for we are all partakers of that one bread." 1 Cor. 10:16, 17.

[227] 1 Cor. 11:23-25; Matt. 26:26-28; Mark 14:22-24; Luke 22:19, 20; 1 Cor. 10:16, 17.

Lord's Day 29

Question 78

Do then the bread and wine become the very body and blood of Christ?

Not at all: [228] but as the water in baptism is not changed into the blood of Christ, neither is the washing away of sin itself, being only the sign and confirmation thereof appointed of God; [229] so the bread in the Lord's supper is not changed into the very body of Christ; [230] though agreeably to the nature and properties of sacraments, [231] it is called the body of Christ Jesus.

[228] Matt. 26:29.
[229] Eph. 5:26; Tit. 3:5.
[230] Mark 14:24; 1 Cor. 10:16, 17, 26-28.
[231] Gen. 17:10, 11, 14, 19; Exod. 12:11, 13, 27, 43, 48; Exod. 13:9; 1 Pet. 3:21; 1 Cor. 10:1-4.

Question 79

Why then doth Christ call the bread "his body", and the cup "his blood", or "the new covenant in his blood"; and Paul the "communion of body and blood of Christ"?

Christ speaks thus, not without great reason, namely, not only thereby to teach us, that as bread and wine support this temporal life, so his crucified body and shed blood are the true meat and drink, whereby our souls are fed to eternal life; [232] but more especially by these visible signs and pledges to assure us, that we are as really partakers of his true body and blood by the operation of the Holy Ghost as we receive by the mouths of our bodies these holy signs in remembrance of him; [233] and that all his sufferings and obedience are as certainly ours, as if we had in our own persons suffered and made satisfaction for our sins to God.

[232] John 6:51, 55.
[233] 1 Cor. 10:16, 17.

Lord's Day 30

Question 80

What difference is there between the Lord's supper and the popish mass?

The Lord's supper testifies to us, that we have a full pardon of all sin by the only sacrifice of Jesus Christ, which he himself has once accomplished on the cross; [234] and, that we by the Holy Ghost are ingrafted into Christ, [235] who, according to his human nature is now not on earth, but in heaven, at the right hand of God his Father, [236] and will there be worshipped by us. [237] But the mass teaches, that the living and dead have not the pardon of sins through the sufferings of Christ, unless Christ is also daily offered for them by the priests; and further, that Christ is bodily under the form of bread and wine, and therefore is to be worshipped in them; so that the mass, at bottom, is nothing else than a denial of the one sacrifice and sufferings of Jesus Christ, and an accursed idolatry. [238]

[234] Heb. 7:27; Heb. 9:12, 25-28; Heb. 10:10, 12-14; John 19:30; Matt. 26:28; Luke 22:19, 20.
[235] 1 Cor. 6:17; 1 Cor. 10:16.
[236] Heb. 1:3; Heb. 8:1, 2; John 20:17.
[237] Matt. 6:20, 21; John 4:21-24; Luke 24:52; Acts 7:55, 56; Col. 3:1; Philip. 3:20, 21; 1 Thess. 1:10; Heb. 9:6-10.
[238] Heb. 9:26; Heb. 10:12, 14, 19-31.

42

Question 81

For whom is the Lord's supper instituted?

For those who are truly sorrowful for their sins, and yet trust that these are forgiven them for the sake of Christ; and that their remaining infirmities are covered by his passion and death; and who also earnestly desire to have their faith more and more strengthened, and their lives more holy; but hypocrites, and such as turn not to God with sincere hearts, eat and drink judgment to themselves. [239]

[239] 1 Cor. 10:19-22; 1 Cor. 11:28, 29.

Question 82

Are they also to be admitted to this supper, who, by confession and life, declare themselves unbelieving and ungodly?

No; for by this, the covenant of God would be profaned, and his wrath kindled against the whole congregation; [240] therefore it is the duty of the christian church, according to the appointment of Christ and his apostles, to exclude such persons, by the keys of the kingdom of heaven, till they show amendment of life.

[240] 1 Cor. 11:20, 34; Isa. 1:11-15; Isa. 66:3; Jer. 7:21-23; Ps. 50:16.

Lord's Day 31

Question 83

What are the keys of the kingdom of heaven?

The preaching of the holy gospel, and christian discipline, or excommunication out of the christian church; by these two, the kingdom of heaven is opened to believers, and shut against unbelievers.
Question 84

How is the kingdom of heaven opened and shut by the preaching of the holy gospel?

Thus: when according to the command of Christ, it is declared and publicly testified to all and every believer, that, whenever they receive the promise of the gospel by a true faith, all their sins are really forgiven them of God, for the sake of Christ's merits; and on the contrary, when it is declared and testified to all unbelievers, and such as do not sincerely repent, that they stand exposed to the wrath of God, and eternal condemnation, so long as they are unconverted: [241] according to which testimony of the gospel, God will judge them, both in this, and in the life to come.

[241] Matt. 16:18, 19; Matt. 18:15-19; John 20:21-23.

Question 85

How is the kingdom of heaven shut and opened by christian discipline?

Thus: when according to the command of Christ, those, who under the name of christians, maintain doctrines, or practices inconsistent therewith, and will not, after having been often brotherly admonished, renounce their errors and wicked course of life, are complained of to the church, or to those, who are thereunto appointed by the church; and if they despise their admonition, are by them forbidden the use of the sacraments; whereby they are excluded from the christian church, and by God himself from the kingdom of Christ; and when they promise and show real amendment, are again received as members of Christ and his church. [242]

[242] Matt. 18:15-18; 1 Cor. 5:2-5, 11; 2 Thess. 3:14, 15; 2 Cor. 2:6-8.

The Third Part--Of Thankfulness

Lord's Day 32

Question 86

Since then we are delivered from our misery, merely of grace, through Christ, without any merit of ours, why must we still do good works?

Because Christ, having redeemed and delivered us by his blood, also renews us by his Holy Spirit, after his own image; that so we may testify, by the whole of our conduct, our gratitude to God for his blessings, [243] and that he may be praised by us; [244] also, that every one may be assured in himself of his faith, [245] by the fruits thereof; and that, by our godly conversation others may be gained to Christ. [246]

[243] Rom. 6:13; Rom. 12:1, 2; 1 Pet. 2:5, 9, 10; 1 Cor. 6:20.
[244] Matt. 5:16; 1 Pet. 2:12; 1 Pet. 1:6 , 7.
[245] 2 Pet. 1:10; Matt. 7:17; Gal. 5:6, 22, 23.
[246] 1 Pet. 3:1, 2; Rom. 14:19.

Question 87

Cannot they then be saved, who, continuing in their wicked and ungrateful lives, are not converted to God?

By no means; for the holy scripture declares that no unchaste person, idolater, adulterer, thief, covetous man, drunkard, slanderer, robber, or any such like, shall inherit the kingdom of God. [247]

[247] 1 Cor. 6:9, 10; Eph. 5:5, 6; 1 John 3:14.

Lord's Day 33

Question 88

Of how many parts does the true conversion of man consist?

Of two parts; of the mortification of the old, and the quickening of the new man. [248]

[248] Rom. 6:1, 4-6; Eph. 4:22-24; Col. 3:5-10; 1 Cor. 5:7; 2 Cor. 7:10.

Question 89

What is the mortification of the old man?

It is a sincere sorrow of heart, that we have provoked God by our sins; and more and more to hate and flee from them. [249]

[249] Rom. 8:13; Joel 2:13; Hos. 6:1.

Question 90

What is the quickening of the new man?

It is a sincere joy of heart in God, through Christ, [250] and with love and delight to live according to the will of God in all good works. [251]

[250] Rom. 5:1; Rom. 14:17; Isa. 57:15.
[251] Rom. 6:10, 11; Gal. 2:20.

Question 91

But what are good works?

Only those which proceed from a true faith, [252] are performed according to the law of God, [253] and to his glory; [254] and not such as are founded on our imaginations, or the institutions of men. [255]

[252] Rom. 14:23.
[253] Lev. 18:4; 1 Sam. 15:22; Eph. 2:10.
[254] 1 Cor. 10:31.
[255] Deut. 12:32; Ezek. 20:18, 19; Isa. 29:13; Matt. 15:7-9.

Lord's Day 34

Question 92

What is the law of God?

God spake all these words, Exodus 20:1-17 and Deuteronomy 5:6-21, saying: I am the LORD thy God, which have brought thee out of the land of Egypt, out of the house of bondage.

1st commandment: Thou shalt have no other gods before me.

2nd commandment: Thou shalt not make unto thee any graven image, or any likeness of any thing that is in heaven above, or that is in the earth beneath, or that is in the water under the earth. Thou shalt not bow down thyself to them, nor serve them; for I the LORD thy God am a jealous God, visiting the iniquity of the fathers upon the children unto the third and fourth generation of them that hate me, and shewing mercy unto thousands of them that love me, and keep my commandments.

3rd commandment: Thou shalt not take the name of the LORD thy God in vain; for the LORD will not hold him guiltless that taketh his name in vain.

4th commandment: Remember the sabbath day, to keep it holy. Six days shalt thou labour, and do all thy work; but the seventh day is the sabbath of the LORD thy God: in it thou shalt not do any work, thou, nor thy son, nor thy daughter, thy manservant, nor thy maidservant, nor thy cattle, nor thy stranger that is within thy gates. For in six days the LORD made heaven and earth, the sea, and all that in them is, and rested the seventh day: wherefore the LORD blessed the sabbath day, and hallowed it.

5th commandment: Honour thy father and thy mother: that thy days may be long upon the land which the LORD thy God giveth thee.

6th commandment: Thou shalt not kill.

7th commandment: Thou shalt not commit adultery.

8th commandment: Thou shalt not steal.

9th commandment: Thou shalt not bear false witness against thy neighbour.

10th commandment: Thou shalt not covet thy neighbour's house, thou shalt not covet thy neighbour's wife, nor his manservant, nor his maid-servant, nor his ox, nor his ass, nor any thing that is thy neighbour's.

Question 93

How are these commandments divided?

Into two tables; [256] the first of which teaches us how we must behave towards God; the second, what duties we owe to our neighbour. [257]

[256] Exod. 34:28; Deut. 4:13; Deut. 10:3, 4.
[257] Matt. 22:37-40.

Question 94

What does God enjoin in the first commandment?

That I, as sincerely as I desire the salvation of my own soul, avoid and flee from all idolatry, [258] sorcery, soothsaying, superstition, [259] invo-cation of saints, or any other creatures; [260] and learn rightly to know the only true God; [261] trust in him alone, [262] with humility [263] and patience submit to him; [264] expect all good things from him only; [265] love, [266] fear, [267] and glorify him with my whole heart; [268] so that I renounce and forsake all creatures, rather than commit even the least thing contrary to his will. [269]

[258] 1 John 5:21; 1 Cor. 6:9, 10; 1 Cor. 10:7, 14.
[259] Lev. 19:31; Deut. 18:9-12.
[260] Matt. 4:10; Rev. 19:10; Rev. 22:8 , 9.
[261] John 17:3.
[262] Jer. 17:5, 7.
[263] 1 Pet. 5:5, 6.
[264] Heb. 10:36; Col. 1:11; Rom. 5:3, 4; 1 Cor. 10:10; Philip. 2:14.
[265] Ps. 104:27-30; Isa. 45:7; James 1:17.

[266] Deut. 6:5; Matt. 22:37.
[267] Deut. 6:2; Ps. 111:10; Prov. 1:7; Prov. 9:10; Matt. 10:28.
[268] Matt. 4:10; Deut. 10:20, 21.
[269] Matt. 5:29, 30; Matt. 10:37; Acts 5:29.

Question 95

What is idolatry?

Idolatry is, instead of, or besides that one true God, who has manifested himself in his word, to contrive, or have any other object, in which men place their trust. [270]

[270] Eph. 5:5; 1 Chron. 16:26; Philip. 3:19; Gal. 4:8; Eph. 2:12; 1 John 2:23; 2 John 1:9; John 5:23.

Lord's Day 35

Question 96

What does God require in the second commandment?

That we in no wise represent God by images, [271] nor worship him in any other way than he has commanded in his word. [272]

[271] Deut. 4:15-19; Isa. 40:18-25; Rom. 1:23, 24; Acts 17:29.
[272] 1 Sam. 15:23; Deut. 12:30-32; Matt. 15:9.

Question 97

Are images then not at all to be made?

God neither can, nor may be represented by any means: [273] but as to creatures; though they may be represented, yet God forbids to make, or have any resemblance of them, either in order to worship them or to serve God by them. [274]

49

[273] Isa. 40:25.
[274] Exod. 23:24, 25; Exod. 34:13, 14, 17; Num. 33:52; Deut. 7:5;
Deut. 12:3; Deut. 16:21; 2 Kin. 18:3, 4.

Question 98

But may not images be tolerated in the churches, as books to the laity?

No: for we must not pretend to be wiser than God, who will have his
people taught, not by dump images, [275] but by the lively preaching of
his word. [276]

[275] Jer. 10:8; Hab. 2:18, 19.
[276] Rom. 10:14, 15, 17; 2 Pet. 1:19; 2 Tim. 3:16, 17.

Lord's Day 36

Question 99

What is required in the third commandment?

That we, not only by cursing [277] or perjury, [278] but also by rash
swearing, [279] must not profane or abuse the name of God; nor by si-
lence or connivance be partakers of these horrible sins in others; [280]
and, briefly, that we use the holy name of God no otherwise than with
fear and reverence; [281] so that he may be rightly confessed [282] and
worshipped by us, [283] and be glorified in all our words and works. [284]

[277] Lev. 24:11-16.
[278] Lev. 19:12.
[279] Matt. 5:37; James 5:12.
[280] Lev. 5:1; Prov. 29:24.
[281] Jer. 4:2; Isa. 45:23.
[282] Rom. 10:9, 10; Matt. 10:32.
[283] Ps. 50:15; 1 Tim. 2:8.
[284] Rom. 2:24; 1 Tim. 6:1; Col. 3:16, 17.

Question 100

Is then the profaning of God's name, by swearing and cursing, so heinous a sin, that his wrath is kindled against those who do not endeavour,
as much as in them lies, to prevent and forbid such cursing and swearing?

It undoubtedly is, [285] for there is no sin greater or more provoking to
God, than the profaning of his name; and therefore he has commanded
this sin to be punished with death. [286]

[285] Prov. 29:24; Lev. 5:1.
[286] Lev. 24:15, 16.

Lord's Day 37

Question 101

May we then swear religiously by the name of God?

Yes: either when the magistrates demand it of the subjects; or when
necessity requires us thereby to confirm a fidelity and truth to the
glory of God, and the safety of our neighbour: for such an oath is
founded on God's word, [287] and therefore was justly used by the
saints, both in the Old and New Testament. [288]

[287] Deut. 6:13; Deut. 10:20; Isa. 48:1 ; Heb. 6:16.
[288] Gen. 21:24; Gen. 31:53, 54; Jos. 9:15, 19; 1 Sam. 24:22; 2 Sam.
3:35; 1 Kin. 1:28-30; Rom. 1:9; 2 Cor. 1:23.

Question 102

May we also swear by saints or any other creatures?

No; for a lawful oath is calling upon God, as the only one who knows
the heart, that he will bear witness to the truth, and punish me if I
swear falsely; [289] which honour is due to no creature. [290]

[289] 2 Cor. 1:23; Rom. 9:1.
[290] Matt. 5:34-36; James 5:12.

Lord's Day 38

Question 103

What does God require in the fourth commandment?

First, that the ministry of the gospel and the schools be maintained; [291] and that I, especially on the sabbath, that is, on the day of rest, diligently frequent the church of God, [292] to hear his word, [293] to use the sacraments, [294] publicly to call upon the Lord, [295] and contribute to the relief of the poor. [296] Secondly, that all the days of my life I cease from my evil works, and yield myself to the Lord, to work by his Holy Spirit in me: and thus begin in this life the eternal sabbath. [297]

[291] Tit. 1:5; 2 Tim. 3:14, 15; 1 Tim. 5:17; 1 Cor. 9:11, 13, 14; 2 Tim. 2:2.
[292] Ps. 40:10, 11; Ps. 68:27; Acts 2:42, 46.
[293] 1 Tim. 4:13, 16; 1 Cor. 14:29, 31.
[294] 1 Cor. 11:33.
[295] 1 Tim. 2:1-3, 8-11; 1 Cor. 14:16.
[296] 1 Cor. 16:2.
[297] Isa. 66:23.

Lord's Day 39

Question 104

What does God require in the fifth commandment?

That I show all honour, love and fidelity, to my father and mother, and all in authority over me, and submit myself to their good instruction and correction, with due obedience; [298] and also patiently bear with their weaknesses and infirmities, [299] since it pleases God to govern us by their hand. [300]

[298] Eph. 5:22; Eph. 6:1-5; Col. 3:18, 20-24; Prov. 1:8; Prov. 4:1; Prov. 15:20; Prov. 20:20; Exod. 21:17; Rom. 13:1-7.
[299] Prov. 23:22; Gen. 9:24, 25; 1 Pet. 2:18.
[300] Eph. 6:4, 9; Col. 3:19-21; Rom. 13:2, 3; Matt. 22:21.

Lord's Day 40

Question 105

What does God require in the sixth commandment?

That neither in thoughts, nor words, nor gestures, much less in deeds, I dishonour, hate, wound, or kill my neighbour, by myself or by another: [301] but that I lay aside all desire of revenge: [302] also, that I hurt not myself, nor wilfully expose myself to any danger. [303] Wherefore also the magistrate is armed with the sword, to prevent murder. [304]

[301] Matt. 5:21, 22; Matt. 26:52; Gen. 9:6.
[302] Eph. 4:26; Rom. 12:19; Matt. 5:25 ; Matt. 18:35.
[303] Rom. 13:14; Col. 2:23; Matt. 4:7.
[304] Gen. 9:6; Exod. 21:14; Matt. 26:52; Rom. 13:4.

Question 106

But this commandment seems only to speak of murder?

In forbidding murder, God teaches us, that he abhors the causes thereof, such as envy, [305] hatred, [306] anger, [307] and desire of revenge; and that he accounts all these as murder. [308]

[305] Prov. 14:30; Rom. 1:29.
[306] 1 John 2:9, 11.
[307] James 1:20; Gal. 5:19, 21.
[308] 1 John 3:15.

Question 107

But is it enough that we do not kill any man in the manner mentioned above?

No: for when God forbids envy, hatred, and anger, he commands us to love our neighbour as ourselves; [309] to show patience, peace, meekness, mercy, and all kindness, towards him, [310] and prevent his hurt as much as in us lies; [311] and that we do good, even to our enemies. [312]

[309] Matt. 7:12; Matt. 22:39; Rom. 12:10.
[310] Eph. 4:2; Gal. 6:1, 2; Matt. 5:5, 7, 9; Rom. 12:18; Luke 6:36; 1 Pet. 3:8; Col. 3:12; Rom. 12:10, 15.
[311] Exod. 23:5.
[312] Matt. 5:44, 45; Rom. 12:20, 21.

Lord's Day 41

Question 108

What does the seventh commandment teach us?

That all uncleanness is accursed of God: [313] and that therefore we must with all our hearts detest the same, [314] and live chastely and temperately, [315] whether in holy wedlock, or in single life. [316]

[313] Lev. 18:27, 28.
[314] Jude 1:23.
[315] 1 Thess. 4:3-5.
[316] Heb. 13:4; 1 Cor. 7:7-9, 27 .

Question 109

Does God forbid in this commandment, only adultery, and such like gross sins?

54

Since both our body and soul are temples of the holy Ghost, he commands us to preserve them pure and holy: therefore he forbids all unchaste actions, gestures, words, [317] thoughts, desires, [318] and whatever can entice men thereto. [319]

[317] Eph. 5:3, 4; 1 Cor. 6:18-20 .
[318] Matt. 5:27, 28.
[319] Eph. 5:18; 1 Cor. 15:33.

Lord's Day 42

Question 110

What does God forbid in the eighth commandment?

God forbids not only those thefts, [320] and robberies, [321] which are punishable by the magistrate; but he comprehends under the name of theft all wicked tricks and devices, whereby we design to appropriate to ourselves the goods which belong to our neighbour: [322] whether it be by force, or under the appearance of right, as by unjust weights, ells, measures, fraudulent merchandise, [323] false coins, usury, [324] or by any other way forbidden by God; as also all covetousness, [325] all abuse and waste of his gifts. [326]

[320] 1 Cor. 6:10.
[321] 1 Cor. 5:10; Isa. 33:1.
[322] Luke 3:14; 1 Thess. 4:6.
[323] Prov. 11:1; Prov. 16:11; Ezek. 45:9-12; Deut. 25:13-16.
[324] Ps. 15:5; Luke 6:35.
[325] 1 Cor. 6:10.
[326] Prov. 23:20, 21; Prov. 21:20.

Question 111

But what does God require in this commandment?

That I promote the advantage of my neighbour in every instance I can or may; and deal with him as I desire to be dealt with by others: [327] further also that I faithfully labour, so that I may be able to relieve the needy. [328]

[327] Matt. 7:12.
[328] Eph. 4:28.

Lord's Day 43

Question 112

What is required in the ninth commandment?

That I bear false witness against no man, [329] nor falsify any man's words; [330] that I be no backbiter, nor slanderer; [331] that I do not judge, nor join in condemning any man rashly, or unheard; [332] but that I avoid all sorts of lies and deceit, as the proper works of the devil, [333] unless I would bring down upon me the heavy wrath of God; [334] likewise, that in judgment and all other dealings I love the truth, speak it uprightly and confess it; [335] also that I defend and promote, as much as I am able, the horror and good character of my neighbour. [336]

[329] Prov. 19:5, 9; Prov. 21:28.
[330] Ps. 15:3; Ps. 50:19, 20.
[331] Rom. 1:29, 30.
[332] Matt. 7:1, 2; Luke 6:37.
[333] John 8:44.
[334] Prov. 12:22; Prov. 13:5.
[335] 1 Cor. 13:6; Eph. 4:25.
[336] 1 Pet. 4:8.

Lord's Day 44

Question 113

What does the tenth commandment require of us?

That even the smallest inclination or thought, contrary to any of God's commandments, never rise in our hearts; but that at all times we hate all sin with our whole heart, and delight in all righteousness. [337]

[337] Rom. 7:7.

Question 114

But can those who are converted to God perfectly keep these commandments?

No: but even the holiest men, while in this life, have only a small beginning of this obedience; [338] yet so, that with a sincere resolution they begin to live, not only according to some, but all the commandments of God. [339]

[338] 1 John 1:8-10; Rom. 7:14, 15; Eccl. 7:20; 1 Cor. 13:9.
[339] Rom. 7:22; Ps. 1:2; James 2:10.

Question 115

Why will God then have the ten commandments so strictly preached, since no man in this life can keep them?

First, that all our lifetime we may learn more and more to know [340] our sinful nature, and thus become the more earnest in seeking the remission of sin, and righteousness in Christ; [341] likewise, that we constantly endeavour and pray to God for the grace of the Holy Spirit, that we may become more and more conformable to the image of God, till we arrive at the perfection proposed to us, in a life to come. [342]

[340] Rom. 3:20; 1 John 1:9; Ps. 32:5.
[341] Matt. 5:6; Rom. 7:24, 25.
[342] 1 Cor. 9:24; Philip. 3:11-14.
Lord's Day 45

Question 116

Why is prayer necessary for christians?

Because it is the chief part of thankfulness which God requires of us: [343] and also, because God will give his grace and Holy Spirit to those only, who with sincere desires continually ask them of him, and are thankful for them. [344]

[343] Ps. 50:14, 15.
[344] Matt. 7:7, 8; Luke 11:9, 10, 13; 1 Thess. 5:17.

Question 117

What are the requisites of that prayer, which is acceptable to God, and which he will hear?

First, that we from the heart pray [345] to the one true God only, who has manifested himself in his word, [346] for all things, he has commanded us to ask of him; [347] secondly, that we rightly and thoroughly know our need and misery, [348] that so we may deeply humble ourselves in the presence of his divine majesty; [349] thirdly, that we be fully persuaded that he, notwithstanding that we are unworthy of it, will, for the sake of Christ our Lord, certainly hear our prayer, [350] as he has promised us in his word. [351]

[345] John 4:24; Ps. 145:18.
[346] Rev. 19:10; John 4:22-24.
[347] Rom. 8:26; 1 John 5:14; James 1:5 .
[348] 2 Chron. 20:12.
[349] Ps. 2:11; Ps. 34:19; Isa. 66:2 .
[350] Rom. 10:14; James 1:6.
[351] John 14:13, 14; John 16:23; Dan. 9:17, 18.

Question 118

What has God commanded us to ask of him?

All things necessary for soul and body; [352] which Christ our Lord has comprised in that prayer he himself has taught us.

[352] James 1:17; Matt. 6:33.

Question 119

What are the words of that prayer? [353]

Our Father which art in heaven, Hallowed be thy name. Thy kingdom come. Thy will be done on earth, as it is in heaven. Give us this day our daily bread. And forgive us our debts, as we forgive our debtors. And lead us not into temptation, but deliver us from evil. For thine is the kingdom, and the power, and the glory, forever. Amen.

[353] Matt. 6:9-13; Luke 11:2-4.

Lord's Day 46

Question 120

Why has Christ commanded us to address God thus: "Our Father"?

That immediately, in the very beginning of our prayer, he might excite in us a childlike reverence for, and confidence in God, which are the foundation of our prayer: namely, that God is become our Father in Christ, and will much less deny us what we ask of him in true faith, than our parents will refuse us earthly things. [354]

[354] Matt. 7:9-11; Luke 11:11-13.

Question 121

Why is it here added, "Which art in heaven"?

Lest we should form any earthly conceptions of God's heavenly majesty, [355] and that we may expect from his almighty power all things necessary for soul and body. [356]

[355] Jer. 23:23, 24; Acts 17:24, 25, 27.
[356] Rom. 10:12.

Lord's Day 47

Question 122

Which is the first petition?

"Hallowed be thy name"; that is, grant us, first, rightly to know thee, [357] and to sanctify, glorify and praise thee, [358] in all thy works, in which thy power, wisdom, goodness, justice, mercy and truth, are clearly displayed; and further also, that we may so order and direct our whole lives, our thoughts, words and actions, that thy name may never be blasphemed, but rather honoured and praised on our account. [359]

[357] John 17:3; Jer. 9:24; Jer. 31:33, 34; Matt. 16:17; James 1:5; Ps. 119:105.
[358] Ps. 119:137; Luke 1:46, 47, 68, 69; Rom. 11:33-36 .
[359] Ps. 71:8; Ps. 115:1.

Lord's Day 48

Question 123

Which is the second petition?

"Thy kingdom come"; that is, rule us so by thy word and Spirit, that we may submit ourselves more and more to thee; [360] preserve and increase thy church; [361] destroy the works of the devil, and all violence which would exalt itself against thee; and also all wicked

counsels devised against thy holy word; [362] till the full perfection of
thy kingdom take place, [363] wherein thou shalt be all in all. [364]

[360] Matt. 6:33; Ps. 119:5; Ps. 143:10 .
[361] Ps. 51:18; Ps. 122:6-9.
[362] 1 John 3:8; Rom. 16:20.
[363] Rev. 22:17, 20; Rom. 8:22, 23.
[364] 1 Cor. 15:28.

Lord's Day 49

Question 124

Which is the third petition?

"Thy will be done on earth as it is in heaven"; that is, grant that we and
all men may renounce our own will, [365] and without murmuring obey
thy will, which is only good; [366] that every one may attend to, and
perform the duties of his station and calling, [367] as willingly and faithfully as the angels do in heaven. [368]

[365] Matt. 16:24; Tit. 2:11, 12.
[366] Luke 22:42; Eph. 5:10; Rom. 12:2 .
[367] 1 Cor. 7:24.
[368] Ps. 103:20, 21.

Lord's Day 50

Question 125

Which is the fourth petition?

"Give us this day our daily bread"; that is, be pleased to provide us
with all things necessary for the body, [369] that we may thereby acknowledge thee to be the only fountain of all good, [370] and that

neither our care nor industry, nor even thy gifts, can profit us without thy blessing; [371] and therefore that we may withdraw our trust from all creatures, and place it alone in thee. [372]

[369] Ps. 104:27, 28; Ps. 145:15, 16; Matt. 6:25, 26.
[370] James 1:17; Acts 14:17; Acts 17:27 , 28.
[371] 1 Cor. 15:58; Deut. 8:3; Ps. 37:3-5, 16; Ps. 127:1, 2.
[372] Ps. 55:23; Ps. 62:11; Ps. 146:3; Jer. 17:5, 7.

Lord's Day 51

Question 126

Which is the fifth petition?

"And forgive us our debts as we forgive our debtors"; that is, be pleased for the sake of Christ's blood, not to impute to us poor sinners, our transgressions, nor that depravity, which always cleaves to us; [373] even as we feel this evidence of thy grace in us, that it is our firm reso-lution from the heart to forgive our neighbour. [374]

[373] Ps. 51:1-7; Ps. 143:2; 1 John 2:1, 2; Rom. 8:1.
[374] Matt. 6:14, 15.

Lord's Day 52

Question 127

Which is the sixth petition?

"And lead us not into temptation, but deliver us from evil"; that is, since we are so weak in ourselves, that we cannot stand a moment; [375] and besides this, since our mortal enemies, the devil, [376] the world, [377] and our own flesh, [378] cease not to assault us, do thou therefore preserve and strengthen us by the power of thy Holy Spirit, that we may not be overcome in this spiritual warfare, [379] but constantly and strenuously may resist our foes, till at last we obtain a complete victory. [380]

[375] John 15:5; Ps. 103:14.
[376] 1 Pet. 5:8; Eph. 6:12.
[377] John 15:19.
[378] Rom. 7:23; Gal. 5:17.
[379] Matt. 26:41; Mark 13:33.
[380] 1 Thess. 3:13; 1 Thess. 5:23.

Question 128

How dost thou conclude thy prayer?

"For thine is the kingdom, and the power, and the glory, forever"; that is, all these we ask of thee, because thou, being our King and almighty, art willing and able to give us all good; [381] and all this we pray for, that thereby not we, but thy holy name, may be glorified for ever. [382]

[381] Rom. 10:11, 12; 2 Pet. 2:9.
[382] John 14:13; Jer. 33:8, 9; Ps. 115:1.

Question 129

What does the word "Amen" signify?

"Amen" signifies, it shall truly and certainly be: for my prayer is more assuredly heard of God, than I feel in my heart that I desire these things of him. [383]

[383] 2 Cor. 1:20; 2 Tim. 2:13.

The Canons of Dordt

First Head of Doctrine

Divine Election and Reprobation

Article 1

As all men have sinned in Adam, lie under the curse, and are deserving of eternal death, God would have done no injustice by leaving them all to perish and delivering them over to condemnation on account of sin, according to the words of the apostle: That every mouth may be stopped, and all the world may be brought under the judgment of God (Rom. 3:19). And: For all have sinned, and fall short of the glory of God (Rom. 3:23). And: For the wages of sin is death (Rom. 6:23).

Article 2

But in this the love of God was manifested, that He sent his only be-gotten Son into the world, that whosoever believeth on him should not perish, but have eternal life (1 John 4:9; John 3:16).

Article 3

And that men may be brought to believe, God mercifully sends the messengers of these most joyful tidings to whom He will and at what time He pleases; by whose ministry men are called to repentance and faith in Christ crucified. How then shall they call on him in whom they have not believed? And how shall they believe in him whom they have not heard? And how shall they hear without a preacher? And how shall they preach except they be sent? (Rom. 10:14, 15).

Article 4

The wrath of God abides upon those who believe not this gospel. But such as receive it and embrace Jesus the Savior by a true and living faith are by Him delivered from the wrath of God and from destruction, and have the gift of eternal life conferred upon them.

Article 5

The cause or guilt of this unbelief as well as of all other sins is no wise in God, but in man himself; whereas faith in Jesus Christ and salvation through Him is the free gift of God, as it is written: By grace have ye been saved through faith; and that not of yourselves, it is the gift of God (Eph. 2:8). Likewise: To you it hath been granted in the behalf of Christ, not only to believe on him, etc. (Phil. 1:29).

Article 6

That some receive the gift of faith from God, and others do not receive it, proceeds from Gods eternal decree. For known unto God are all his works from the beginning of the world (Acts 15:18, A.V.). Who worketh all things after the counsel of his will (Eph. 1:11). According to which decree He graciously softens the hearts of the elect, however obstinate, and inclines them to believe; while He leaves the non- elect in His just judgment to their own wickedness and obduracy. And herein is especially displayed the profound, the merciful, and at the same time the righteous discrimination between men equally involved in ruin; or that decree of election and reprobation, revealed in the Word of God, which, though men of perverse, impure, and unstable minds wrest it to their own destruction, yet to holy and pious souls affords unspeakable consolation.

Article 7

Election is the unchangeable purpose of God, whereby, before the foundation of the world, He has out of mere grace, according to the sovereign good pleasure of His own will, chosen from the whole human race, which had fallen through their own fault from their primitive state of rectitude into sin and destruction, a certain number of persons to redemption in Christ, whom He from eternity appointed the Mediator and Head of the elect and the foundation of salvation. This elect number, though by nature neither better nor more deserving than others, but with them involved in one common misery, God has decreed to give to Christ to be saved by Him, and effectually to call and draw them to His communion by His Word and Spirit; to bestow upon them true faith, justification, and sanctification; and having powerfully preserved them in the fellowship of His Son, finally to glorify them for the demonstration of His mercy, and for the praise of the riches of His glorious grace; as it is written: Even as he chose us in him before the foundation of the world, that we should be holy and without blemish before him in love: having foreordained us unto adoption as sons through Jesus Christ unto himself, according to the good pleasure of his will, to the praise of the glory of his grace, which he freely bestowed on us in the Beloved (Eph. 1:4, 5, 6). And elsewhere: Whom he foreordained, them he also called: and whom he called, them he also justified: and whom he justified, them he also glorified (Rom. 8:30).

Article 8

There are not various decrees of election, but one and the same decree respecting all those who shall be saved, both under the Old and the New Testament; since the Scripture declares the good pleasure, purpose, and counsel of the divine will to be one, according to which He has chosen us from eternity, both to grace and to glory, to salvation and to the way of salvation, which He has ordained that we should walk therein (Eph. 1:4, 5; 2:10).

Article 9

This election was not founded upon foreseen faith and the obedience of faith, holiness, or any other good quality or disposition in man, as the prerequisite, cause, or condition on which it depended; but men are chosen to faith and to the obedience of faith, holiness, etc. Therefore election is the fountain of every saving good, from which proceed faith, holiness, and the other gifts of salvation, and finally eternal life itself, as its fruits and effects, according to the testimony of the apostle: He hath chosen us (not because we were, but) that we should be holy, and without blemish before him in love (Eph. 1:4).

Article 10

The good pleasure of God is the sole cause of this gracious election; which does not consist herein that out of all possible qualities and actions of men God has chosen some as a condition of salvation, but that He was pleased out of the common mass of sinners to adopt some certain persons as a peculiar people to Himself, as it is written: For the children being not yet born, neither having done anything good or bad, etc., it was said unto her (namely, to Rebekah), The elder shall serve the younger. Even as it is written, Jacob I loved, but Esau I hated (Rom. 9:11, 12, 13). And as many as were ordained to eternal life believed (Acts 13:48).

Article 11

And as God Himself is most wise, unchangeable, omniscient, and omnipotent, so the election made by Him can neither be interrupted nor changed, recalled, or annulled; neither can the elect be cast away, nor their number diminished.

Article 12

The elect in due time, though in various degrees and in different measures, attain the assurance of this their eternal and unchangeable election, not by inquisitively prying into the secret and deep things of God, but by observing in themselves with a spiritual joy and holy pleasure the infallible fruits of election pointed out in the Word of God such as, a true faith in Christ, filial fear, a godly sorrow for sin, a hungering and thirsting after righteousness, etc.

Article 13

The sense and certainty of this election afford to the children of God additional matter for daily humiliation before Him, for adoring the depth of His mercies, for cleansing themselves, and rendering grateful returns of ardent love to Him who first manifested so great love towards them. The consideration of this doctrine of election is so far from encouraging remissness in the observance of the divine commands or from sinking men in carnal security, that these, in the just judgment of God, are the usual effects of rash presumption or of idle and wanton trifling with the grace of election, in those who refuse to walk in the ways of the elect.

Article 14

As the doctrine of divine election by the most wise counsel of God was declared by the prophets, by Christ Himself, and by the apostles, and is clearly revealed in the Scriptures both of the Old and the New Testament, so it is still to be published in due time and place in the Church of God, for which it was peculiarly designed, provided it be done with reverence, in the spirit of discretion and piety, for the glory of Gods most holy Name, and for enlivening and comforting His people, without vainly attempting to investigate the secret ways of the Most High (Acts 20:27; Rom. 11:33, 34; 12:3; Heb. 6:17, 18).

Article 15

What peculiarly tends to illustrate and recommend to us the eternal and unmerited grace of election is the express testimony of sacred Scripture that not all, but some only, are elected, while others are passed by in the eternal decree; whom God, out of His sovereign, most just, irreprehensible, and unchangeable good pleasure, has decreed to leave in the common misery into which they have wilfully plunged themselves, and not to bestow upon them saving faith and the grace of conversion; but, permitting them in His just judgment to follow their own ways, at last, for the declaration of His justice, to condemn and punish them forever, not only on account of their unbelief, but also for all their other sins. And this is the decree of reprobation, which by no means makes God the Author of sin (the very thought of which is blasphemy), but declares Him to be an awful, irreprehensible, and righteous Judge and Avenger thereof.

Article 16

Those in whom a living faith in Christ, an assured confidence of soul, peace of conscience, an earnest endeavor after filial obedience, a glorying in God through Christ, is not as yet strongly felt, and who nevertheless make use of the means which God has appointed for working these graces in us, ought not to be alarmed at the mention of reprobation, nor to rank themselves among the reprobate, but diligently to persevere in the use of means, and with ardent desires devoutly and humbly to wait for a season of richer grace. Much less cause to be terrified by the doctrine of reprobation have they who, though they seriously desire to be turned to God, to please Him only, and to be delivered from the body of death, cannot yet reach that measure of holiness and faith to which they aspire; since a merciful God has promised that He will not quench the smoking flax, nor break the bruised reed. But this doctrine is justly terrible to those who, regardless of God and of the Savior Jesus Christ, have wholly given themselves up to the cares of the world and the pleasures of the flesh, so long as they are not seriously converted to God.

Article 17

Since we are to judge of the will of God from His Word, which testifies that the children of believers are holy, not by nature, but in virtue of the covenant of grace, in which they together with the parents are comprehended, godly parents ought not to doubt the election and salvation of their children whom it pleases God to call out of this life in their infancy (Gen. 17:7; Acts 2:39; 1 Cor. 7:14).

Article 18

To those who murmur at the free grace of election and the just severity of reprobation we answer with the apostle: Nay but, O man, who art thou that repliest against God? (Rom. 9:20), and quote the language of our Savior: Is it not lawful for me to do what I will with mine own? (Matt. 20:15). And therefore, with holy adoration of these mysteries, we exclaim in the words of the apostle: O the depth of the riches both of the wisdom and the knowledge of God! how unsearchable are his judgments, and his ways past tracing out! For who hath known the mind of the Lord, or who hath been his counsellor? or who hath first given to him, and it shall be recompensed unto him again? For of him, and through him, and unto him are all things. To him be the glory for ever. Amen. (Rom. 11:33-36).

Rejection of Errors

The true doctrine concerning election and reprobation having been explained, the Synod rejects the errors of those:

Paragraph 1

Who teach: That the will of God to save those who would believe and would persevere in faith and in the obedience of faith is the whole and entire decree of election unto salvation, and that nothing else concerning this decree has been revealed in Gods Word.

For these deceive the simple and plainly contradict the Scriptures, which declare that God will not only save those who will believe, but that He has also from eternity chosen certain particular persons to whom, above others, He will grant, in time, both faith in Christ and perseverance; as it is written: I manifested thy name unto the men whom thou gavest me out of the world (John 17:6). And as many as were ordained to eternal life believed (Acts 13:48). And: Even as he chose us in him before the foundation of the world, that we should be holy and without blemish before him in love (Eph. 1:4).

Paragraph 2

Who teach: That there are various kinds of election of God unto eternal life: the one general and indefinite, the other particular and definite; and that the latter in turn is either incomplete, revocable, non-decisive, and conditional, or complete, irrevocable, decisive, and absolute. Likewise: That there is one election unto faith and another unto salvation, so that election can be unto justifying faith, without being a decisive election unto salvation.

For this is a fancy of mens minds, invented regardless of the Scriptures, whereby the doctrine of election is corrupted, and this golden chain of our salvation is broken: And whom he foreordained, them he also called: and whom he called, them he also justified: and whom he justified, them he also glorified (Rom. 8:30).

Paragraph 3

Who teach: That the good pleasure and purpose of God, of which Scripture makes mention in the doctrine of election, does not consist in this, that God chose certain persons rather than others, but in this, that He chose out of all possible conditions (among which are also the works of the law), or out of the whole order of things, the act of faith which from its very nature is undeserving, as well as its incomplete obedience, as a condition of salvation, and that He would graciously consider this in itself as a complete obedience and count it worthy of the reward of eternal life.

For by this injurious error the pleasure of God and the merits of Christ are made of none effect, and men are drawn away by useless questions from the truth of gracious justification and from the simplicity of Scripture, and this declaration of the apostle is charged as untrue: Who saved us, and called us with a holy calling, not according to our works, but according to his own purpose and grace, which was given us in Christ Jesus before times eternal (2 Tim. 1:9).

Paragraph 4

Who teach: That in the election unto faith this condition is beforehand demanded that man should use his innate understanding of God aright, be pious, humble, meek, and fit for eternal life, as if on these things election were in any way dependent.

For this savors of the teaching of Pelagius, and is opposed to the doctrine of the apostle when he writes: Among whom we also all once lived in the lust of our flesh, doing the desires of the flesh and of the mind, and were by nature children of wrath, even as the rest; but God, being rich in mercy, for his great love wherewith he loved us, even when we were dead through our trespasses, made us alive together with Christ (by grace have ye been saved), and raised us up with him, and made us to sit with him in the heavenly places, in Christ Jesus; that in the ages to come he might show the exceeding riches of his grace in kindness towards us in Christ Jesus; for by grace have ye been saved through faith; and that not of yourselves, it is the gift of God; not of works, that no man should glory (Eph. 2:3-9).

Paragraph 5

Who teach: That the incomplete and non-decisive election of particular persons to salvation occurred because of a foreseen faith, conversion, holiness, godliness, which either began or continued for some time; but that the complete and decisive election occurred because of foreseen perseverance unto the end in faith, conversion, holiness, and godliness; and that this is the gracious and evangelical worthiness, for the sake of which he who is chosen is more worthy than he who is not chosen; and that therefore faith, the obedience of faith, holiness, godliness, and perseverance are not fruits of the unchangeable election unto glory, but are conditions which, being required beforehand, were foreseen as being met by those who will be fully elected, and are causes without which the unchangeable election to glory does not occur.

This is repugnant to the entire Scripture, which constantly inculcates this and similar declara tions: Election is not of works, but of him that calleth (Rom. 9:11). And as many as were ordained to eternal life believed (Acts 13:48). He chose us in him before the foundation of the world, that we should be holy (Eph. 1:4). Ye did not choose me, but I chose you (John 15:16). But if it is by grace, it is no more of works (Rom. 11:6). Herein is love, not that we loved God, but that he loved us, and sent his Son (1 John 4:10).

Paragraph 6

Who teach: That not every election unto salvation is unchangeable, but that some of the elect, any decree of God notwithstanding, can yet perish and do indeed perish.

By this gross error they make God to be changeable, and destroy the comfort which the godly obtain out of the firmness of their election, and contradict the Holy Scripture, which teaches that the elect can not be led astray (Matt. 24:24), that Christ does not lose those whom the Father gave him (John 6:39), and that God also glorified those whom he foreordained, called, and justified (Rom. 8:30).

Paragraph 7

Who teach: That there is in this life no fruit and no consciousness of the unchangeable election to glory, nor any certainty, except that which depends on a changeable and uncertain condition.

For not only is it absurd to speak of an uncertain certainty, but also contrary to the experience of the saints, who by virtue of the consciousness of their election rejoice with the apostle and praise this favor of God (Eph. 1); who according to Christs admonition rejoice with his disciples that their names are written in heaven (Luke 10:20); who also place the consciousness of their election over against the fiery darts of the devil, asking: Who shall lay anything to the charge of Gods elect? (Rom. 8:33).

Paragraph 8

Who teach: That God, simply by virtue of His righteous will, did not decide either to leave anyone in the fall of Adam and in the common state of sin and condemnation, or to pass anyone by in the communication of grace which is necessary for faith and conversion.

For this is firmly decreed: He hath mercy on whom he will, and whom he will he hardeneth (Rom. 9:18). And also this: Unto you it is given to know the mysteries of the kingdom of heaven, but to them it is not given (Matt. 13:11). Likewise: I thank thee, O Father, Lord of heaven and earth, that thou didst hide these things from the wise and understanding, and didst reveal them unto babes; yea, Father, for so it was well-pleasing in thy sight (Matt. 11:25, 26).

Paragraph 9

Who teach: That the reason why God sends the gospel to one people rather than to another is not merely and solely the good pleasure of God, but rather the fact that one people is better and worthier than another to which the gospel is not communicated.

For this Moses denies, addressing the people of Israel as follows: Behold, unto Jehovah thy God belongeth heaven and the heaven of heavens, the earth, with all that is therein. Only Jehovah had a delight in thy fathers to love them, and he chose their seed after them, even you above all peoples, as at this day(Deut. 10:14, 15). And Christ said: Woe unto thee, Chorazin! woe unto thee, Bethsaida! for if the mighty works had been done in Tyre and Sidon which were done in you, they would have repented long ago in sackcloth and ashes (Matt. 11:21).

Second Head of Doctrine

The Death of Christ, and the Redemption of Men Thereby

Article 1

God is not only supremely merciful, but also supremely just. And His justice requires (as He has revealed Himself in His Word) that our sins committed against His infinite majesty should be punished, not only with temporal but with eternal punishments, both in body and soul; which we cannot escape, unless satisfaction be made to the justice of God.

Article 2

Since, therefore, we are unable to make that satisfaction in our own persons, or to deliver ourselves from the wrath of God, He has been pleased of His infinite mercy to give His only begotten Son for our Surety, who was made sin, and became a curse for us and in our stead, that He might make satisfaction to divine justice on our behalf.

Article 3

The death of the Son of God is the only and most perfect sacrifice and satisfaction for sin, and is of infinite worth and value, abundantly sufficient to expiate the sins of the whole world.

Article 4

This death is of such infinite value and dignity because the person who submitted to it was not only really man and perfectly holy, but also the only begotten Son of God, of the same eternal and infinite essence with the Father and the Holy Spirit, which qualifications were necessary to constitute Him a Savior for us; and, moreover, because it was attended with a sense of the wrath and curse of God due to us for sin.

Article 5

Moreover, the promise of the gospel is that whosoever believes in Christ crucified shall not perish, but have eternal life. This promise, together with the command to repent and believe, ought to be declared and published to all nations, and to all persons promiscuously and without distinction, to whom God out of His good pleasure sends the gospel.

Article 6

And, whereas many who are called by the gospel do not repent nor believe in Christ, but perish in unbelief, this is not owing to any defect or insufficiency in the sacrifice offered by Christ upon the cross, but is wholly to be imputed to themselves.

Article 7

But as many as truly believe, and are delivered and saved from sin and destruction through the death of Christ, are indebted for this benefit solely to the grace of God given them in Christ from everlasting, and not to any merit of their own.

Article 8

For this was the sovereign counsel and most gracious will and purpose of God the Father that the quickening and saving efficacy of the most precious death of His Son should extend to all the elect, for bestowing upon them alone the gift of justifying faith, thereby to bring them infallibly to salvation; that is, it was the will of God that Christ by the blood of the cross, whereby He confirmed the new covenant, should effectually redeem out of every people, tribe, nation, and language, all those, and those only, who were from eternity chosen to salvation and given to Him by the Father; that He should confer upon them faith, which, together with all the other saving gifts of the Holy Spirit, He purchased for them by His death; should purge them from all sin, both original and actual, whether committed before or after believing; and having faithfully preserved them even to the end, should at last bring them, free from every spot and blemish, to the enjoyment of glory in His own presence forever.

Article 9

This purpose, proceeding from everlasting love towards the elect, has from the beginning of the world to this day been powerfully accomplished, and will henceforward still continue to be accomplished, notwithstanding all the ineffectual opposition of the gates of hell; so that the elect in due time may be gathered together into one, and that there never may be wanting a Church composed of believers, the foundation of which is laid in the blood of Christ; which may steadfastly love and faithfully serve Him as its Savior (who, as a bridegroom for his bride, laid down His life for them upon the cross); and which may celebrate His praises here and through all eternity.

Rejection of Errors

The true doctrine having been explained, the Synod rejects the errors of those:

Paragraph 1

Who teach: That God the Father has ordained His Son to the death of the cross without a certain and definite decree to save any, so that the necessity, profitableness, and worth of what Christ merited by His death might have existed, and might remain in all its parts complete, perfect, and intact, even if the merited redemption had never in fact been applied to any person.

For this doctrine tends to the despising of the wisdom of the Father and of the merits of Jesus Christ, and is contrary to Scripture. For thus says our Savior: I lay down my life for the sheep, and I know them (John 10:15, 27). And the prophet Isaiah says concerning the Savior: When thou shalt make his soul an offering for sin, he shall see his seed, he shall prolong his days, and the pleasure of Jehovah shall prosper in his hand (Is. 53:10). Finally, this contradicts the article of faith according to which we believe the catholic Christian Church.

Paragraph 2

Who teach: That it was not the purpose of the death of Christ that He should confirm the new covenant of grace through His blood, but only that He should acquire for the Father the mere right to establish with man such a covenant as He might please, whether of grace or of works.

For this is repugnant to Scripture which teaches that Christ hath become the surety and mediator of a better, that is, the new covenant, and that a testament is of force where there hath been death (Heb. 7:22; 9:15, 17).

Paragraph 3

Who teach: That Christ by His satisfaction merited neither salvation itself for anyone, nor faith, whereby this satisfaction of Christ unto salvation is effectually appropriated; but that He merited for the Father only the authority or the perfect will to deal again with man, and to prescribe new conditions as He might desire, obedience to which, however, depended on the free will of man, so that it therefore might have come to pass that either none or all should fulfill these conditions.

For these adjudge too contemptuously of the death of Christ, in no wise acknowledge the most important fruit or benefit thereby gained, and bring again out of hell the Pelagian error.

Paragraph 4

Who teach: That the new covenant of grace, which God the Father, through the mediation of the death of Christ, made with man, does not herein consist that we by faith, inasmuch as it accepts the merits of Christ, are justified before God and saved, but in the fact that God, having revoked the demand of perfect obedience of faith, regards faith itself and the obedience of faith, although imperfect, as the perfect obedience of the law, and does esteem it worthy of the reward of eternal life through grace.

For these contradict the Scriptures: Being justified freely by his grace through the redemption that is in Christ Jesus; whom God set forth to be a propitiation, through faith, in his blood (Rom. 3:24, 25). And these proclaim, as did the wicked Socinus, a new and strange justification of man before God, against the consensus of the whole Church.

Paragraph 5

Who teach: That all men have been accepted unto the state of reconciliation and unto the grace of the covenant, so that no one is worthy of condemnation on account of original sin, and that no one shall be condemned because of it, but that all are free from the guilt of original sin.

For this opinion is repugnant to Scripture which teaches that we are by nature children of wrath (Eph. 2:3).

Paragraph 6

Who use the difference between meriting and appropriating, to the end that they may instil into the minds of the imprudent and inexperienced this teaching that God, as far as He is concerned, has been minded to apply to all equally the benefits gained by the death of Christ; but that, while some obtain the pardon of sin and eternal life, and others do not, this difference depends on their own free will, which joins itself to the grace that is offered without exception, and that it is not dependent on the special gift of mercy, which powerfully works in them, that they rather than others should appropriate unto themselves this grace.

For these, while they feign that they present this distinction in a sound sense, seek to instil into the people the destructive poison of the Pelagian errors.

Paragraph 7

Who teach: That Christ neither could die, nor needed to die, and also did not die, for those whom God loved in the highest degree and elected to eternal life, since these do not need the death of Christ.

For they contradict the apostle, who declares: Christ loved me, and gave himself up for me (Gal. 2:20). Likewise: Who shall lay anything to the charge of Gods elect? It is God that justifieth; who is he that condemneth? It is Christ Jesus that died (Rom. 8:33, 34), namely, for them; and the Savior who says: I lay down my life for the sheep (John 10:15). And: This is my commandment, that ye love one another, even as I have loved you. Greater love hath no man than this, that a man lay down his life for his friends (John 15:12, 13).

Third and Fourth Heads of Doctrine

The Corruption of Man, His Conversion to God, and the Manner Thereof

Article 1

Man was originally formed after the image of God. His understanding was adorned with a true and saving knowledge of his Creator, and of spiritual things; his heart and will were upright, all his affections pure, and the whole man was holy. But, revolting from God by the instigation of the devil and by his own free will, he forfeited these excellent gifts; and in the place thereof became involved in blindness of mind, horrible darkness, vanity, and perverseness of judgment; became wicked, rebellious, and obdurate in heart and will, and impure in his affections.

Article 2

Man after the fall begat children in his own likeness. A corrupt stock produced a corrupt offspring. Hence all the posterity of Adam, Christ only excepted, have derived corruption from their original parent, not by imitation, as the Pelagians of old asserted, but by the propagation of a vicious nature, in consequence of the just judgment of God.

Article 3

Therefore all men are conceived in sin, and are by nature children of wrath, incapable of saving good, prone to evil, dead in sin, and in bondage thereto; and without the regenerating grace of the Holy Spirit, they are neither able nor willing to return to God, to reform the depravity of their nature, or to dispose themselves to reformation.

Article 4

There remain, however, in man since the fall, the glimmerings of natural understanding, whereby he retains some knowledge of God, of natural things, and of the difference between good and evil, and shows some regard for virtue and for good outward behavior. But so far is this understanding of nature from being sufficient to bring him to a saving knowledge of God and to true conversion that he is incapable of using it aright even in things natural and civil. Nay further, this understanding, such as it is, man in various ways renders wholly polluted, and hinders in unrighteousness, by doing which he becomes inexcusable before God.

Article 5

Neither can the decalogue delivered by God to His peculiar people, the Jews, by the hands of Moses, save men. For though it reveals the greatness of sin, and more and more convinces man thereof, yet, as it neither points out a remedy nor imparts strength to extricate him from this misery, but, being weak through the flesh, leaves the transgressor under the curse, man cannot by this law obtain saving grace.

Article 6

What, therefore, neither the innate understanding nor the law could do, that God performs by the operation of the Holy Spirit through the word or ministry of reconciliation; which is the glad tidings concerning the Messiah, by means whereof it has pleased God to save such as believe, as well under the Old as under the New Testament.

Article 7

This mystery of His will God revealed to but a small number under the Old Testament; under the New Testament (the distinction between various peoples having been removed) He reveals it to many. The cause of this dispensation is not to be ascribed to the superior worth of one nation above another, nor to their better use of the innate understanding of God, but results wholly from the sovereign good pleasure and unmerited love of God. Hence they to whom so great and so gracious a blessing is communicated, above their desert, or rather notwithstanding their demerits, are bound to acknowledge it with humble and grateful hearts, and with the apostle to adore, but in no wise curiously to pry into, the severity and justice of God's judgments displayed in others to whom this grace is not given.

Article 8

As many as are called by the gospel are unfeignedly called. For God has most earnestly and truly declared in His Word what is acceptable to Him, namely, that those who are called should come unto Him. He also seriously promises rest of soul and eternal life to all who come to Him and believe.

Article 9

It is not the fault of the gospel, nor of Christ offered therein, nor of God, who calls men by the gospel and confers upon them various gifts, that those who are called by the ministry of the Word refuse to come and be converted. The fault lies in themselves; some of whom when called, regardless of their danger, reject the Word of life; others, though they receive it, suffer it not to make a lasting impression on their heart; therefore, their joy, arising only from a temporary faith, soon vanishes, and they fall away; while others choke the seed of the Word by perplexing cares and the pleasures of this world, and produce no fruit. This our Savior teaches in the parable of the sower (Matt. 13).

Article 10

But that others who are called by the gospel obey the call and are converted is not to be ascribed to the proper exercise of free will, whereby one distinguishes himself above others equally furnished with grace sufficient for faith and conversion (as the proud heresy of Pelagius maintains); but it must be wholly ascribed to God, who, as He has chosen His own from eternity in Christ, so He calls them effectually in time, confers upon them faith and repentance, rescues them from the power of darkness, and translates them into the kingdom of His own Son; that they may show forth the praises of Him who has called them out of darkness into His marvelous light, and may glory not in themselves but in the Lord, according to the testimony of the apostles in various places.

Article 11

But when God accomplishes His good pleasure in the elect, or works in them true conversion, He not only causes the gospel to be externally preached to them, and powerfully illuminates their minds by His Holy Spirit, that they may rightly understand and discern the things of the Spirit of God; but by the efficacy of the same regenerating Spirit He pervades the inmost recesses of man; He opens the closed and softens the hardened heart, and circumcises that which was uncircumcised; infuses new qualities into the will, which, though heretofore dead, He quickens; from being evil, disobedient, and refractory, He renders it good, obedient, and pliable; actuates and strengthens it, that like a good tree, it may bring forth the fruits of good actions.

Article 12

And this is that regeneration so highly extolled in Scripture, that renewal, new creation, resurrection from the dead, making alive, which God works in us without our aid. But this is in no wise effected merely by the external preaching of the gospel, by moral suasion, or such a mode of operation that, after God has performed His part, it still remains in the power of man to be regenerated or not, to be converted or to continue unconverted; but it is evidently a supernatural work, most powerful, and at the same time most delightful, astonishing, mysterious, and ineffable; not inferior in efficacy to creation or the resurrection from the dead, as the Scripture inspired by the Author of this work declares; so that all in whose heart God works in this marvelous manner are certainly, infallibly, and effectually regenerated, and do actually believe. Whereupon the will thus renewed is not only actuated and influenced by God, but in consequence of this influence becomes itself active. Wherefore also man himself is rightly said to believe and repent by virtue of that grace received.

Article 13

The manner of this operation cannot be fully comprehended by believers in this life. Nevertheless, they are satisfied to know and experience that by this grace of God they are enabled to believe with the heart and to love their Savior.

Article 14

Faith is therefore to be considered as the gift of God, not on account of its being offered by God to man, to be accepted or rejected at his pleasure, but because it is in reality conferred upon him, breathed and infused into him; nor even because God bestows the power or ability to believe, and then expects that man should by the exercise of his own free will consent to the terms of salvation and actually believe in Christ, but because He who works in man both to will and to work, and indeed all things in all, produces both the will to believe and the act of believing also.

Article 15

God is under no obligation to confer this grace upon any; for how can He be indebted to one who had no previous gifts to bestow as a foundation for such recompense? Nay, how can He be indebted to one who has nothing of his own but sin and falsehood? He, therefore, who becomes the subject of this grace owes eternal gratitude to God, and gives Him thanks forever. Whoever is not made partaker thereof is either altogether regardless of these spiritual gifts and satisfied with his own condition, or is in no apprehension of danger, and vainly boasts the possession of that which he has not. Further, with respect to those who outwardly profess their faith and amend their lives, we are bound, after the example of the apostle, to judge and speak of them in the most favorable manner; for the secret recesses of the heart are unknown to us. And as to others who have not yet been called, it is our duty to pray for them to God, who calls the things that are not as if they were. But we are in no wise to conduct ourselves towards them with haughtiness, as if we had made ourselves to differ.

Article 16

But as man by the fall did not cease to be a creature endowed with understanding and will, nor did sin which pervaded the whole race of mankind deprive him of the human nature, but brought upon him depravity and spiritual death; so also this grace of regeneration does not treat men as senseless stocks and blocks, nor take away their will and its properties, or do violence thereto; but it spiritually quickens, heals, corrects, and at the same time sweetly and powerfully bends it, that where carnal rebellion and resistance formerly prevailed, a ready and sincere spiritual obedience begins to reign; in which the true and spiritual restoration and freedom of our will consist. Wherefore, unless the admirable Author of every good work so deal with us, man can have no hope of being able to rise from his fall by his own free will, by which, in a state of innocence, he plunged himself into ruin.

Article 17

As the almighty operation of God whereby He brings forth and supports this our natural life does not exclude but require the use of means by which God, of His infinite mercy and goodness, has chosen to exert His influence, so also the aforementioned supernatural operation of God by which we are regenerated in no wise excludes or subverts the use of the gospel, which the most wise God has ordained to be the seed of regeneration and food of the soul. Wherefore, as the apostles and the teachers who succeeded them piously instructed the people concerning this grace of God, to His glory and to the abasement of all pride, and in the meantime, however, neglected not to keep them, by the holy admonitions of the gospel, under the influence of the Word, the sacraments, and ecclesiastical discipline; so even now it should be far from those who give or receive instruction in the Church to presume to tempt God by separating what He of His good pleasure has most intimately joined together. For grace is conferred by means of admonitions; and the more readily we perform our duty, the more clearly this favor of God, working in us, usually manifests itself, and the more directly His work is advanced; to whom alone all the glory, both for the means and for their saving fruit and efficacy, is forever due.
Amen.

Rejection of Errors

The true doctrine having been explained, the Synod rejects the errors of those:

Paragraph 1

Who teach: That it cannot properly be said that original sin in itself suffices to condemn the whole human race or to deserve temporal and eternal punishment.

For these contradict the apostle, who declares: Therefore, as through one man sin entered into the world, and death through sin; and so death passed unto all men, for that all sinned (Rom. 5:12). And: The judgment came of one unto condemnation (Rom. 5:16). And: The wages of sin is death (Rom. 6:23).

Paragraph 2

Who teach: That the spiritual gifts or the good qualities and virtues, such as goodness, holiness, righteousness, could not belong to the will of man when he was first created, and that these, therefore, cannot have been separated therefrom in the fall.

For such is contrary to the description of the image of God which the apostle gives in Eph. 4:24, where he declares that it consists in righteousness and holiness, which undoubtedly belong to the will.

Paragraph 3

Who teach: That in spiritual death the spiritual gifts are not separate from the will of man, since the will in itself has never been corrupted, but only hindered through the darkness of the understanding and the irregularity of the affections; and that, these hindrances having been removed, the will can then bring into operation its native powers, that is, that the will of itself is able to will and to choose, or not to will and not to choose, all manner of good which may be presented to it.

This is an innovation and an error, and tends to elevate the powers of the free will, contrary to the declaration of the prophet: The heart is deceitful above all things, and it is exceedingly corrupt (Jer. 17:9); and of the apostle: Among whom (sons of disobedience) we also all once lived in the lusts of our flesh, doing the desires of the flesh and of the mind (Eph. 2:3).

Paragraph 4

Who teach: That the unregenerate man is not really nor utterly dead in sin, nor destitute of all powers unto spiritual good, but that he can yet hunger and thirst after righteousness and life, and offer the sacrifice of a contrite and broken spirit, which is pleasing to God.

For these things are contrary to the express testimony of Scripture: Ye were dead through your trespasses and sins (Eph. 2:1, 5). And: Every imagination of the thoughts of his heart was only evil continually (Gen. 6:5; 8:21). Moreover, to hunger and thirst after deliverance from misery and after life, and to offer unto God the sacrifice of a broken spirit, is peculiar to the regenerate and those that are called blessed (Ps. 51:17; Matt. 5:6).

Paragraph 5

Who teach: That the corrupt and natural man can so well use the common grace (by which they understand the light of nature), or the gifts still left him after the fall, that he can gradually gain by their good use a greater, that is, the evangelical or saving grace, and salvation itself; and that in this way God on His part shows Himself ready to reveal Christ unto all men, since He applies to all sufficiently and effi- ciently the means necessary to conversion.

For both the experience of all ages and the Scriptures testify that this is untrue. He showeth his word unto Jacob, his statutes and his ordin- ances unto Israel. He hath not dealt so with any nation; and as for his ordinances, they have not known them (Ps. 147:19, 20). Who in the generations gone by suffered all the nations to walk in their own way (Acts 14:16). And: And they (Paul and his companions) having been forbidden of the Holy Spirit to speak the word in Asia, when they were come over against Mysia, they assayed to go into Bithynia, and the Spirit of Jesus suffered them not (Acts 16:6, 7).

Paragraph 6

Who teach: That in the true conversion of man no new qualities, pow- ers, or gifts can be infused by God into the will, and that therefore faith, through which we are first converted and because of which we are called believers, is not a quality or gift infused by God but only an act of man, and that it cannot be said to be a gift, except in respect of the power to attain to this faith.

For thereby they contradict the Holy Scriptures, which declare that God infuses new qualities of faith, of obedience, and of the consciousness of His love into our hearts: I will put my law in their inward parts, and in their heart will I write it (Jer. 31:33). And: I will pour water upon him that is thirsty, and streams upon the dry ground; I will pour my Spirit upon thy seed (Is. 44:3). And: The love of God hath been shed abroad in our hearts through the Holy Spirit which was given unto us (Rom. 5:5). This is also repugnant to the constant practice of the Church, which prays by the mouth of the prophet thus: Turn thou me, and I shall be turned (Jer. 31:18).

Paragraph 7

Who teach: That the grace whereby we are converted to God is only a gentle advising, or (as others explain it) that this is the noblest manner of working in the conversion of man, and that this manner of working, which consists in advising, is most in harmony with mans nature; and that there is no reason why this advising grace alone should not be sufficient to make the natural man spiritual; indeed, that God does not produce the consent of the will except through this manner of advising; and that the power of the divine working, whereby it surpasses the working of Satan, consists in this that God promises eternal, while Satan promises only temporal goods.

But this is altogether Pelagian and contrary to the whole Scripture, which, besides this, teaches yet another and far more powerful and divine manner of the Holy Spirits working in the conversion of man, as in Ezekiel: A new heart also will I give you, and a new spirit will I put within you; and I will take away the stony heart out of your flesh, and I will give you a heart of flesh (Ezek. 36:26).

Paragraph 8

Who teach: That God in the regeneration of man does not use such powers of His omnipotence as potently and infallibly bend mans will to faith and conversion; but that all the works of grace having been accomplished, which God employs to convert man, man may yet so resist God and the Holy Spirit, when God intends mans regeneration and wills to regenerate him, and indeed that man often does so resist that he prevents entirely his regeneration, and that it therefore remains in mans power to be regenerated or not.

For this is nothing less than the denial of all the efficiency of Gods grace in our conversion, and the subjecting of the working of Almighty God to the will of man, which is contrary to the apostles, who teach that we believe according to the working of the strength of his might (Eph. 1:19); and that God fulfills every desire of goodness and every work of faith with power (2 Thess. 1:11); and that his divine power hath granted unto us all things that pertain unto life and godliness (2 Peter 1:3).

Paragraph 9

Who teach: That grace and free will are partial causes which together work the beginning of conversion, and that grace, in order of working, does not precede the working of the will; that is, that God does not efficiently help the will of man unto conversion until the will of man moves and determines to do this.

For the ancient Church has long ago condemned this doctrine of the Pelagians according to the words of the apostle: So then it is not of him that willeth, nor of him that runneth, but of God that hath mercy (Rom. 9:16). Likewise: For who maketh thee to differ? and what hast thou that thou didst not receive? (1 Cor. 4:7). And: For it is God who worketh in you both to will and to work, for his good pleasure (Phil. 2:13).

Fifth Head of Doctrine

The Perseverance of the Saints

Article 1

Those whom God, according to His purpose, calls to the communion of His Son, our Lord Jesus Christ, and regenerates by the Holy Spirit, He also delivers from the dominion and slavery of sin, though in this life He does not deliver them altogether from the body of sin and from the infirmities of the flesh.

Article 2

Hence spring forth the daily sins of infirmity, and blemishes cleave even to the best works of the saints. These are to them a perpetual reason to humiliate themselves before God and to flee for refuge to Christ crucified; to mortify the flesh more and more by the spirit of prayer and by holy exercises of piety; and to press forward to the goal of perfection, until at length, delivered from this body of death, they shall reign with the Lamb of God in heaven.

Article 3

By reason of these remains of indwelling sin, and also because of the temptations of the world and of Satan, those who are converted could not persevere in that grace if left to their own strength. But God is faithful, who, having conferred grace, mercifully confirms and powerfully preserves them therein, even to the end.

Article 4

Although the weakness of the flesh cannot prevail against the power of God, who confirms and preserves true believers in a state of grace, yet converts are not always so influenced and actuated by the Spirit of God as not in some particular instances sinfully to deviate from the guidance of divine grace, so as to be seduced by and to comply with the lusts of the flesh; they must, therefore, be constant in watching and prayer, that they may not be led into temptation. When these are neglected, they are not only liable to be drawn into great and heinous sins by the flesh, the world, and Satan, but sometimes by the righteous permission of God actually are drawn into these evils. This, the lamentable fall of David, Peter, and other saints described in Holy Scripture, demonstrates.

Article 5

By such enormous sins, however, they very highly offend God, incur a deadly guilt, grieve the Holy Spirit, interrupt the exercise of faith, very grievously wound their consciences, and sometimes for a while lose the sense of Gods favor, until, when they change their course by serious repentance, the light of Gods fatherly countenance again shines upon them.

Article 6

But God, who is rich in mercy, according to His unchangeable purpose of election, does not wholly withdraw the Holy Spirit from His own people even in their grievous falls; nor suffers them to proceed so far as to lose the grace of adoption and forfeit the state of justification, or to commit the sin unto death or against the Holy Spirit; nor does He permit them to be totally deserted, and to plunge themselves into everlasting destruction.

Article 7

For in the first place, in these falls He preserves in them the incorruptible seed of regeneration from perishing or being totally lost; and again, by His Word and Spirit He certainly and effectually renews them to repentance, to a sincere and godly sorrow for their sins, that they may seek and obtain remission in the blood of the Mediator, may again experience the favor of a reconciled God, through faith adore His mercies, and henceforward more diligently work out their own salvation with fear and trembling.

Article 8

Thus it is not in consequence of their own merits or strength, but of Gods free mercy, that they neither totally fall from faith and grace nor continue and perish finally in their backslidings; which, with respect to themselves is not only possible, but would undoubtedly happen; but with respect to God, it is utterly impossible, since His counsel cannot be changed nor His promise fail; neither can the call according to His purpose be revoked, nor the merit, inter- cession, and preservation of Christ be rendered ineffectual, nor the sealing of the Holy Spirit be frustrated or obliterated.

Article 9

Of this preservation of the elect to salvation and of their perseverance in the faith, true believers themselves may and do obtain assurance according to the measure of their faith, whereby they surely believe that they are and ever will continue true and living members of the Church, and that they have the forgiveness of sins and life eternal.

Article 10

This assurance, however, is not produced by any peculiar revelation contrary to or independent of the Word of God, but springs from faith in Gods promises, which He has most abundantly revealed in His Word for our comfort; from the testimony of the Holy Spirit, witness-ing with our spirit that we are children and heirs of God (Rom. 8:16); and lastly, from a serious and holy desire to preserve a good con-science and to perform good works. And if the elect of God were deprived of this solid comfort that they shall finally obtain the victory, and of this infallible pledge of eternal glory, they would be of all men the most miserable.

Article 11

The Scripture moreover testifies that believers in this life have to struggle with various carnal doubts, and that under grievous tempta-tions they do not always feel this full assurance of faith and certainty of persevering. But God, who is the Father of all consolation, does not suffer them to be tempted above that they are able, but will with the temptation make also the way of escape, that they may be able to endure it (1 Cor. 10:13), and by the Holy Spirit again inspires them with the comfortable assurance of persevering.

Article 12

This certainty of perseverance, however, is so far from exciting in believers a spirit of pride, or of rendering them carnally secure, that on the contrary it is the real source of humility, filial reverence, true piety, patience in every tribulation, fervent prayers, constancy in suffering and in confessing the truth, and of solid rejoicing in God; so that the consideration of this benefit should serve as an incentive to the serious and constant practice of gratitude and good works, as appears from the testimonies of Scripture and the examples of the saints.

Article 13

Neither does renewed confidence of persevering produce licentiousness or a disregard of piety in those who are recovered from backsliding; but it renders them much more careful and solicitous to continue in the ways of the Lord, which He has ordained, that they who walk therein may keep the assurance of persevering; lest, on account of their abuse of His fatherly kindness, God should turn away His gracious countenance from them (to behold which is to the godly dearer than life, and the withdrawal of which is more bitter than death) and they in consequence thereof should fall into more grievous torments of conscience.

Article 14

And as it has pleased God, by the preaching of the gospel, to begin this work of grace in us, so He preserves, continues, and perfects it by the hearing and reading of His Word, by meditation thereon, and by the exhortations, threatenings, and promises thereof, and by the use of the sacraments.

Article 15

The carnal mind is unable to comprehend this doctrine of the perseverance of the saints and the certainty thereof, which God has most abundantly revealed in His Word, for the glory of His Name and the consolation of pious souls, and which He impresses upon the hearts of the believers. Satan abhors it, the world ridicules it, the ignorant and hypocritical abuse it, and the heretics oppose it. But the bride of Christ has always most tenderly loved and constantly defended it as an inestimable treasure; and God, against whom neither counsel nor strength can prevail, will dispose her so to continue to the end. Now to this one God, Father, Son, and Holy Spirit, be honor and glory forever. Amen.

Rejection of Errors

The true doctrine having been explained, the Synod rejects the errors of those:

Paragraph 1

Who teach: That the perseverance of the true believers is not a fruit of election, or a gift of God gained by the death of Christ, but a condition of the new covenant, which (as they declare) man before his decisive election and justification must fulfil through his free will.

For the Holy Scripture testifies that this follows out of election, and is given the elect in virtue of the death, the resurrection, and intercession of Christ: But the election obtained it, and the rest were hardened (Rom. 11:7). Likewise: He that spared not his own Son, but delivered him up for us all, how shall he not also with him freely give us all things? Who shall lay anything to the charge of Gods elect? It is God that justifieth; who is he that condemneth? It is Christ Jesus that died, yea rather, that was raised from the dead, who is at the right hand of God, who also maketh intercession for us. Who shall separate us from the love of Christ? (Rom. 8:32-35).

Paragraph 2

Who teach: That God does indeed provide the believer with sufficient powers to persevere, and is ever ready to preserve these in him if he will do his duty; but that, though all things which are necessary to persevere in faith and which God will use to preserve faith are made use of, even then it ever depends on the pleasure of the will whether it will persevere or not.

For this idea contains an outspoken Pelagianism, and while it would make men free, it makes them robbers of Gods honor, contrary to the prevailing agreement of the evangelical doctrine, which takes from man all cause of boasting, and ascribes all the praise for this favor to the grace of God alone; and contrary to the apostle, who declares that it is God, who shall also confirm you unto the end, that ye be unreprovable in the day of our Lord Jesus Christ (1 Cor. 1:8).

Paragraph 3

Who teach: That the true believers and regenerate not only can fall from justifying faith and likewise from grace and salvation wholly and to the end, but indeed often do fall from this and are lost forever.

For this conception makes powerless the grace, justification, regeneration, and continued preservation by Christ, contrary to the expressed words of the apostle Paul: That, while we were yet sinners, Christ died for us. Much more then, being now justified by his blood, shall we be saved from the wrath of God through him (Rom. 5:8, 9). And contrary to the apostle John: Whosoever is begotten of God doeth no sin, because his seed abideth in him; and he can not sin, because he is begotten of God (1 John 3:9). And also contrary to the words of Jesus Christ: I give unto them eternal life; and they shall never perish, and no one shall snatch them out of my hand. My Father, who hath given them to me, is greater than all; and no one is able to snatch them out of the Fathers hand (John 10:28, 29).

Paragraph 4

Who teach: That true believers and regenerate can sin the sin unto death or against the Holy Spirit.

Since the same apostle John, after having spoken in the fifth chapter of his first epistle, vs. 16 and 17, of those who sin unto death and having forbidden to pray for them, immediately adds to this in vs. 18: We know that whosoever is begotten of God sinneth not (meaning a sin of that character), but he that was begotten of God keepeth himself, and the evil one toucheth him not (1 John 5:18).

Paragraph 5

Who teach: That without a special revelation we can have no certainty of future perseverance in this life.

For by this doctrine the sure comfort of the true believers is taken away in this life, and the doubts of the papist are again introduced into the Church, while the Holy Scriptures constantly deduce this assurance, not from a special and extraordinary revelation, but from the marks proper to the children of God and from the very constant promises of God. So especially the apostle Paul: No creature shall be able to separate us from the love of God, which is in Christ Jesus our Lord (Rom. 8:39). And John declares: And he that keepeth his commandments abideth in him, and he in him. And hereby we know that he abideth in us, by the Spirit which he gave us (1 John 3:24).

Paragraph 6

Who teach: That the doctrine of the certainty of perseverance and of salvation from its own character and nature is a cause of indolence and is injurious to godliness, good morals, prayers, and other holy exercises, but that on the contrary it is praiseworthy to doubt.

For these show that they do not know the power of divine grace and the working of the indwelling Holy Spirit. And they contradict the apostle John, who teaches the opposite with express words in his first epistle: Beloved, now are we children of God, and it is not yet made manifest what we shall be. We know that, if he shall be manifested, we shall be like him; for we shall see him even as he is. And every one that hath this hope set on him purifieth himself, even as he is pure (1 John 3:2, 3). Furthermore, these are contradicted by the example of the saints, both of the Old and the New Testament, who though they were assured of their perseverance and salvation, were nevertheless constant in prayers and other exercises of godliness.

Paragraph 7

Who teach: That the faith of those who believe for a time does not differ from justifying and saving faith except only in duration.

For Christ Himself, in Matt. 13:20, Luke 8:13, and in other places, evidently notes, besides this duration, a threefold difference between those who believe only for a time and true believers, when He declares that the former receive the seed in stony ground, but the latter in the good ground or heart; that the former are without root, but the latter have a firm root; that the former are without fruit, but that the latter bring forth their fruit in various measure, with constancy and steadfastness.

Paragraph 8

Who teach: That it is not absurd that one having lost his first regeneration is again and even often born anew.

For these deny by this doctrine the incorruptibleness of the seed of God, whereby we are born again; contrary to the testimony of the apostle Peter: Having been begotten again, not of corruptible seed, but of incorruptible (1 Peter 1:23).

Paragraph 9

Who teach: That Christ has in no place prayed that believers should infallibly continue in faith.

For they contradict Christ Himself, who says: I made supplication for thee (Simon), that thy faith fail not (Luke 22:32), and the evangelist John, who declares that Christ has not prayed for the apostles only, but also for those who through their word would believe: Holy Father, keep them in thy name, and: I pray not that thou shouldest take them from the world, but that thou shouldest keep them from the evil one(John 17:11, 15, 20).

Conclusion

And this is the perspicuous, simple, and ingenuous declaration of the orthodox doctrine respecting the five articles which have been controverted in the Belgic Churches; and the rejection of the errors, with which they have for some time been troubled. This doctrine the Synod judges to be drawn from the Word of God, and to be agreeable to the confession of the Reformed Churches. Whence it clearly appears that some, whom such conduct by no means became, have violated all truth, equity, and charity, in wishing to persuade the public:

That the doctrine of the Reformed Churches concerning predestination, and the points annexed to it, by its own genius and necessary tendency, leads off the minds of men from all piety and religion; that it is an opiate administered by the flesh and the devil; and the stronghold of Satan, where he lies in wait for all, and from which he wounds multitudes, and mortally strikes through many with the darts both of despair and security; that it makes God the author of sin, unjust, tyrannical, hypocritical; that it is nothing more than an interpolated Stoicism, Manicheism, Libertinism, Turcism; that it renders men carnally secure, since they are persuaded by it that nothing can hinder the salvation of the elect, let them live as they please; and, therefore, that they may safely perpetrate every species of the most atrocious crimes; and that, if the reprobate should even perform truly all the works of the saints, their obedience would not in the least contribute to their salvation; that the same doctrine teaches that God, by a mere arbitrary act of his will, without the least respect or view to any sin, has predestinated the greatest part of the world to eternal damnation, and has created them for this very purpose; that in the same manner in which the election is the fountain and cause of faith and good works, reprobation is the cause of unbelief and impiety; that many children of the faithful are torn, guiltless, from their mothers breasts, and tyrannically plunged into hell: so that neither baptism nor the prayers of the Church at their baptism can at all profit them ; and many other things of the same kind which the Reformed Churches not only do not acknowledge, but even detest with their whole soul.

Wherefore, this Synod of Dort, in the name of the Lord, conjures as many as piously call upon the name of our Savior Jesus Christ to judge of the faith of the Reformed Churches, not from the calumnies which on every side are heaped upon it, nor from the private expressions of a few among ancient and modern teachers, often dishonestly quoted, or corrupted and wrested to a meaning quite foreign to their intention; but from the public confessions of the Churches themselves, and from this declaration of the orthodox doctrine, confirmed by the unanimous consent of all and each of the members of the whole Synod. Moreover, the Synod warns calumniators themselves to consider the terrible judgment of God which awaits them, for bearing false witness against the confessions of so many Churches; for distressing the consciences of the weak; and for laboring to render suspected the society of the truly faithful.

Finally, this Synod exhorts all their brethren in the gospel of Christ to conduct themselves piously and religiously in handling this doctrine, both in the universities and churches; to direct it, as well in discourse as in writing, to the glory of the Divine name, to holiness of life, and to the consolation of afflicted souls; to regulate, by the Scripture, according to the analogy of faith, not only their sentiments, but also their language, and to abstain from all those phrases which exceed the limits necessary to be observed in ascertaining the genuine sense of the Holy Scriptures, and may furnish insolent sophists with a just pretext for violently assailing, or even vilifying, the doctrine of the Reformed Churches. May Jesus Christ, the Son of God, who, seated at the Fathers right hand, gives gifts to men, sanctify us in the truth; bring to the truth those who err; shut the mouths of the calumniators of sound doctrine, and endue the faithful ministers of his Word with the spirit of wisdom and discretion, that all their discourses may tend to the glory of God, and the edification of those who hear them. Amen.

The Belgic Confession

The Belgic Confession was originally composed in 1561 by Guido de Bres for the churches in Flanders and the Netherlands. It was adopted by a Reformed Synod at Emden, in 1571. During the Synod of Dordt in 1618-1619, several editions of the Confession in differing languages (French, Dutch, and Latin) were carefully examined and an official, revised edition was produced. According to Schaff, "It is, upon the whole, the best symbolical statement of the Calvinistic system of doctrine, with the exception of the Westminster Confession." [385]

Article I

There Is Only One God

We all believe with the heart and confess with the mouth that there is one only simple and spiritual Being, which we call God; and that He is eternal, incomprehensible, invisible, immutable, infinite, almighty, perfectly wise, just, good, and the overflowing fountain of all good.

Article II

By What Means God Is Made Known unto Us

We know Him by two means: First, by the creation, preservation, and government of the universe; which is before our eyes as a most elegant book, wherein all creatures, great and small, are as so many characters leading us to see clearly the invisible things of God, even his everlasting power and divinity, as the apostle Paul says (Rom. 1:20). All which things are sufficient to convince men and leave them without excuse. Second, He makes Himself more clearly and fully known to us by His holy and divine Word, that is to say, as far as is necessary for us to know in this life, to His glory and our salvation.

Article III

The Written Word of God

We confess that this Word of God was not sent nor delivered by the will of man, but that men spake from God, being moved by the Holy Spirit, as the apostle Peter says; and that afterwards God, from a special care which He has for us and our salvation, commanded His servants, the prophets and apostles, to commit His revealed word to writing; and He Himself wrote with His own finger the two tables of the law. Therefore we call such writings holy and divine Scriptures.

Article IV

Canonical Books of the Holy Scripture

We believe that the Holy Scriptures are contained in two books, namely, the Old and the New Testament, which are canonical, against which nothing can be alleged. These are thus named in the Church of God.

The books of the Old Testament are the five books of Moses, to wit: Genesis, Exodus, Leviticus, Numbers, Deuteronomy; the book of Joshua, Judges, Ruth, the two books of Samuel, the two of the Kings, two books of the Chronicles, Ezra, Nehemiah, Esther; Job, the Psalms, the three books of Solomon, namely, the Proverbs, Ecclesiastes, and the Song of Songs; the four great prophets, Isaiah, Jeremiah (Lamentations), Ezekiel, and Daniel; and the twelve lesser prophets, namely, Hosea, Joel, Amos, Obadiah, Jonah, Micah, Nahum, Habakkuk, Zephaniah, Haggai, Zechariah, and Malachi.

Those of the New Testament are the four evangelists, to wit: Matthew, Mark, Luke, and John; the Acts of the Apostles; the thirteen epistles of the apostle Paul, namely, one to the Romans, two to the Corinthians, one to the Galatians, one to the Ephesians, one to the Philippians, one to the Colossians, two to the Thessalonians, two to Timothy, one to Titus, one to Philemon; Hebrews; the seven epistles of the other apostles, namely, one of James, two of Peter, three of John, one of Jude; and the Revelation of the apostle John.

Article V

Whence the Holy Scriptures Derive Their Dignity and Authority

We receive all these books, and these only, as holy and canonical, for the regulation, foundation, and confirmation of our faith; believing without any doubt all things contained in them, not so much because the Church receives and approves them as such, but more especially because the Holy Spirit witnesses in our hearts that they are from God, and also because they carry the evidence thereof in themselves. For the very blind are able to perceive that the things foretold in them are being fulfilled.

Article VI

The Difference Between the Canonical and Apocryphal Books

We distinguish those sacred books from the apocryphal, viz: the third and fourth books of Esdras, the books of Tobit, Judith, Wisdom, Jesus Sirach, Baruch, the Appendix to the book of Esther, the Song of the Three Children in the Furnace, the History of Susannah, of Bel and the Dragon, the Prayer of Manasseh, and the two books of the Maccabees. All of which the Church may read and take instruction from, so far as they agree with the canonical books; but they are far from having such power and efficacy that we may from their testimony confirm any point of faith or of the Christian religion; much less may they be used to detract from the authority of the other, that is, the sacred books.

Article VII

The Sufficiency of the Holy Scriptures to Be the Only Rule of Faith

We believe that those Holy Scriptures fully contain the will of God, and that whatsoever man ought to believe unto salvation is sufficiently taught therein. For since the whole manner of worship which God requires of us is written in them at large, it is unlawful for any one, though an apostle, to teach otherwise than we are now taught in the Holy Scriptures: nay, though it were an angel from heaven, as the apostle Paul says. For since it is forbidden to add unto or take away anything from the Word of God, it does thereby evidently appear that the doctrine thereof is most perfect and complete in all respects.

Neither may we consider any writings of men, however holy these men may have been, of equal value with those divine Scriptures, nor ought we to consider custom, or the great multitude, or antiquity, or succession of times and persons, or councils, decrees or statutes, as of equal value with the truth of God, since the truth is above all; for all men are of themselves liars, and more vain than vanity itself. Therefore we reject with all our hearts whatsoever does not agree with this infallible rule, as the apostles have taught us, saying, Prove the spirits, whether they are of God. Likewise: If any one cometh unto you, and bringeth not this teaching, receive him not into your house.

Article VIII

God Is One in Essence, Yet Distinguished in Three Persons

According to this truth and this Word of God, we believe in one only God, who is the one single essence, in which are three persons, really, truly, and eternally distinct according to their incommunica ble properties; namely, the Father, and the Son, and the Holy Spirit. The Father is the cause, origin, and beginning of all things visible and invisible; the Son is the word, wisdom, and image of the Father; the Holy Spirit is the eternal power and might, proceeding from the Father and the Son. Nevertheless, God is not by this distinction divided into three, since the Holy Scriptures teach us that the Father, and the Son, and the Holy Spirit have each His personality, distinguished by Their properties; but in such wise that these three persons are but one only God.

Hence, then, it is evident that the Father is not the Son, nor the Son the Father, and likewise the Holy Spirit is neither the Father nor the Son. Nevertheless, these persons thus distinguished are not divided, nor intermixed; for the Father has not assumed the flesh, nor has the Holy Spirit, but the Son only. The Father has never been without His Son, or without His Holy Spirit. For They are all three co- eternal and co-essential. There is neither first nor last; for They are all three one, in truth, in power, in goodness, and in mercy.

Article IX

The Proof of the Foregoing Article of the Trinity of Persons in One God

All this we know as well from the testimonies of Holy Writ as from their operations, and chiefly by those we feel in ourselves. The testimonies of the Holy Scriptures that teach us to believe this Holy Trinity are written in many places of the Old Testament, which are not so necessary to enumerate as to choose them out with discretion and judgment.

In Genesis, chap. 1:26, 27, God says: Let us make man in our image, after our likeness, etc. And God created man in his own image, male and female created he them. And Gen. 3:22 , Behold, the man is become as one of us. From this saying, Let us make man in our image, it appears that there are more persons than one in the Godhead; and when He says, God created, He signifies the unity. It is true, He does not say how many persons there are, but that which appears to us somewhat obscure in the Old Testament is very plain in the New. For when our Lord was baptized in Jordan, the voice of the Father was heard, saying, This is my beloved Son; the Son was seen in the water, and the Holy Spirit appeared in the shape of a dove. This form is also instituted by Christ in the baptism of all believers: Make disciples of all the nations, baptizing them into the name of the Father and of the Son and of the Holy Spirit. In the Gospel of Luke the angel Gabriel thus addressed Mary, the mother of our Lord: The Holy Spirit shall come upon thee, and the power of the Most High shall overshadow thee; wherefore also the holy thing which is begotten shall be called the Son of God. Likewise: The grace of the Lord Jesus Christ, and the love of God, and the communion of the Holy Spirit, be with you all. And (A.V.): There are three that bear record in heaven, the Father, the Word, and the Holy Ghost: and these three are one.

In all these places we are fully taught that there are three persons in one only divine essence. And although this doctrine far surpasses all human understanding, nevertheless we now believe it by means of the Word of God, but expect hereafter to enjoy the perfect knowledge and benefit thereof in heaven.

Moreover, we must observe the particular offices and operations of these three persons towards us. The Father is called our Creator, by His power; the Son is our Savior and Redeemer, by His blood; the Holy Spirit is our Sanctifier, by His dwelling in our hearts.

This doctrine of the Holy Trinity has always been affirmed and maintained by the true Church since the time of the apostles to this very day against the Jews, Mohammedans, and some false Christians and heretics, as Marcion, Manes, Praxeas, Sabellius, Samosatenus, Arius, and such like, who have been justly condemned by the orthodox fathers. Therefore, in this point, we do willingly receive the three creeds, namely, that of the Apostles, of Nicea, and of Athanasius; likewise that which, conformable thereunto, is agreed upon by the ancient fathers.

Article X

Jesus Christ Is True and Eternal God

We believe that Jesus Christ according to His divine nature is the only begotten Son of God, begotten from eternity, not made, nor created (for then He would be a creature), but co-essential and co- eternal with the Father, the very image of his substance and the effulgence of his glory, equal unto Him in all things. He is the Son of God, not only from the time that He assumed our nature but from all eternity, as these testimonies, when compared together, teach us. Moses says that God created the world; and St. John says that all things were made by that Word which he calls God. The apostle says that God made the world by His Son; likewise, that God created all things by Jesus Christ. Therefore it must needs follow that He who is called God, the Word, the Son, and Jesus Christ, did exist at that time when all things were created by Him. Therefore the prophet Micah says: His goingsforth are from of old, from everlasting. And the apostle: He hath

106

neither beginning of days nor end of life. He therefore is that true, eternal, and almighty God whom we invoke, worship, and serve.

Article XI

The Holy Spirit Is True and Eternal God

We believe and confess also that the Holy Spirit from eternity proceeds from the Father and the Son; and therefore neither is made, created, nor begotten, but only proceeds from both; who in order is the third person of the Holy Trinity; of one and the same essence, majesty, and glory with the Father and the Son; and therefore is the true and eternal God, as the Holy Scriptures teach us.

Article XII

The Creation of All Things, Especially the Angels

We believe that the Father by the Word, that is, by His Son, has created of nothing the heaven, the earth, and all creatures, when it seemed good unto Him; giving unto every creature its being, shape, form, and several offices to serve its Creator; that He also still upholds and governs them by His eternal providence and infinite power for the service of mankind, to the end that man may serve his God.
He also created the angels good, to be His messengers and to serve His elect; some of whom are fallen from that excellency in which God created them into everlasting perdition, and the others have by the grace of God remained steadfast and continued in their first state. The devils and evil spirits are so depraved that they are enemies of God and every good thing; to the utmost of their power as murderers watching to ruin the Church and every member thereof, and by their wicked stratagems to destroy all; and are, therefore, by their own wickedness adjudged to eternal damnation, daily expecting their horrible torments.

Therefore we reject and abhor the error of the Sadducees, who deny the existence of spirits and angels; and also that of the Manichees, who assert that the devils have their origin of themselves, and that they are wicked of their own nature, without having been corrupted.

Article XIII

The Providence of God and His Government of All Things

We believe that the same good God, after He had created all things, did not forsake them or give them up to fortune or chance, but that He rules and governs them according to His holy will, so that nothing happens in this world without His appointment; nevertheless, God neither is the Author of nor can be charged with the sins which are committed. For His power and goodness are so great and incomprehensible that He orders and executes His work in the most excellent and just manner, even then when devils and wicked men act unjustly. And as to what He does surpassing human understanding, we will not curiously inquire into farther than our capacity will admit of; but with the greatest humility and reverence adore the righteous judgments of God, which are hid from us, contenting ourselves that we are pupils of Christ, to learn only those things which He has revealed to us in His Word, without transgress ing these limits.

This doctrine affords us unspeakable consolation, since we are taught thereby that nothing can befall us by chance, but by the direction of our most gracious and heavenly Father; who watches over us with a paternal care, keeping all creatures so under His power that not a hair of our head (for they are all numbered), nor a sparrow can fall to the ground without the will of our Father, in whom we do entirely trust; being persuaded that He so restrains the devil and all our enemies that without His will and permission they cannot hurt us.

And therefore we reject that damnable error of the Epicureans, who say that God regards nothing but leaves all things to chance.

Article XIV

The Creation and Fall of Man, and His Incapacity to Perform What Is Truly Good

We believe that God created man out of the dust of the earth, and made and formed him after His own image and likeness, good, righteous, and holy, capable in all things to will agreeably to the will of God. But being in honor, he understood it not, neither knew his excellency, but wilfully subjected himself to sin and consequently to death and the curse, giving ear to the words of the devil. For the command ment of life, which he had received, he transgressed; and by sin separated himself from God, who was his true life; having corrupted his whole nature; whereby he made himself liable to corporal and spiritual death. And being thus become wicked, perverse, and corrupt in all his ways, he has lost all his excellent gifts which he had received from God, and retained only small remains thereof, which, however, are sufficient to leave man without excuse; for all the light which is in us is changed into darkness, as the Scriptures teach us, saying: The light shineth in the darkness, and the darkness apprehended it not; where St. John calls men darkness.

Therefore we reject all that is taught repugnant to this concerning the free will of man, since man is but a slave to sin, and can receive nothing, except it have been given him from heaven. For who may presume to boast that he of himself can do any good, since Christ says: No man can come to me, except the Father that sent me draw him? Who will glory in his own will, who understands that the mind of the flesh is enmity against God? Who can speak of his knowledge, since the natural man receiveth not the things of the Spirit of God? In short, who dares suggest any thought, since he knows that we are not sufficient of ourselves to account anything as of ourselves, but that our sufficiency is of God? And therefore what the apostle says ought justly to be held sure and firm, that God worketh in us both to will and to work, for his good pleasure. For there is no understanding nor will conformable to the divine understand ing and will but what Christ has wrought in man; which He teaches us, when He says: Apart from me ye can do nothing.

Article XV

Original Sin

We believe that through the disobedience of Adam original sin is extended to all mankind; which is a corruption of the whole nature and a hereditary disease, wherewith even infants in their mothers womb are infected, and which produces in man all sorts of sin, being in him as a root thereof, and therefore is so vile and abominable in the sight of God that it is sufficient to condemn all mankind. Nor is it altogether abolished or wholly eradicated even by regeneration; since sin always issues forth from this woeful source, as water from a fountain; notwithstanding it is not imputed to the children of God unto condemnation, but by His grace and mercy is forgiven them. Not that they should rest securely in sin, but that a sense of this corruption should make believers often to sigh, desiring to be delivered from this body of death.

Wherefore we reject the error of the Pelagians, who assert that sin proceeds only from imitation.

Article XVI

Eternal Election

We believe that, all the posterity of Adam being thus fallen into perdition and ruin by the sin of our first parents, God then did manifest Himself such as He is; that is to say, merciful and just; merciful, since He delivers and preserves from this perdition all whom He in His eternal and unchangeable counsel of mere goodness has elected in Christ Jesus our Lord, without any respect to their works; just, in leaving others in the fall and perdition wherein they have involved themselves.

Article XVII

The Recovery of Fallen Man

We believe that our most gracious God, in His admirable wisdom and goodness, seeing that man had thus thrown himself into physical and spiritual death and made himself wholly miserable, was pleased to seek and comfort him, when he trembling fled from His presence, promising him that He would give His Son (who would be born of a woman) to bruise the head of the serpentand to make him blessed.

Article XVIII

The Incarnation of Jesus Christ

We confess, therefore, that God has fulfilled the promise which He made to the fathers by the mouth of His holy prophets, when He sent into the world, at the time appointed by Him, His own only- begotten and eternal Son, who took upon Him the form of a servant and became like unto man, really assuming the true human nature with all its infirmities, sin excepted; being conceived in the womb of the blessed virgin Mary by the power of the Holy Spirit without the means of man; and did not only assume human nature as to the body, but also a true human soul, that He might be a real man. For since the soul was lost as well as the body, it was necessary that He should take both upon Him, to save both.

Therefore we confess (in opposition to the heresy of the Anabaptists, who deny that Christ assumed human flesh of His mother) that Christ partook of the flesh and blood of the children; that He is a fruit of the loins of David after the flesh; born of the seed of David according to the flesh; a fruit of the womb of Mary; born of a woman; a branch of David; a shoot of the root of Jesse; sprung from the tribe of Judah; descended from the Jews according to the flesh; of the seed of Abraham, since (A.V.) he took on him the seed of Abraham, and was made like unto his brethren in all things, sin excepted; so that in truth He is our IMMANUEL, that is to say, God with us.

Article XIX

The Union and Distinction of the Two Natures in the Person of Christ

We believe that by this conception the person of the Son is inseparably united and connected with the human nature; so that there are not two Sons of God, nor two persons, but two natures united in one single person; yet each nature retains its own distinct properties. As, then, the divine nature has always remained uncreated, without beginning of days or end of life, filling heaven and earth, so also has the human nature not lost its properties but remained a creature, having beginning of days, being a finite nature, and retaining all the properties of a real body. And though He has by His resurrection given immortality to the same, nevertheless He has not changed the reality of His human nature; forasmuch as our salvation and resurrection also depend on the reality of His body. But these two natures are so closely united in one person that they were not separated even by His death. Therefore that which He, when dying, commended into the hands of His Father, was a real human spirit, departing from His body. But in the meantime the divine nature always remained united with the human, even when He lay in the grave; and the Godhead did not cease to be in Him, any more than it did when He was an infant, though it did not so clearly manifest itself for a while. Wherefore we confess that He is very God and very man: very God by His power to conquer death; and very man that He might die for us according to the infirmity of His flesh.

Article XX

God Has Manifested His Justice and Mercy in Christ

We believe that God, who is perfectly merciful and just, sent His Son to assume that nature in which the disobedience was committed, to make satisfaction in the same, and to bear the punishment of sin by His most bitter passion and death. God therefore manifested His justice against His Son when He laid our iniquities upon Him, and poured forth His mercy and goodness on us, who were guilty and worthy of damnation, out of mere and perfect love, giving His Son unto death for us, and raising Him for our justification, that through Him we might obtain immortality and life eternal.

Article XXI

The Satisfaction of Christ, Our Only High Priest, for Us

We believe that Jesus Christ is ordained with an oath to be an everlasting High Priest, after the order of Melchizedek; and that He has presented Himself in our behalf before the Father, to appease His wrath by His full satisfaction, by offering Himself on the tree of the cross, and pouring out His precious blood to purge away our sins, as the prophets had foretold. For it is written: He was wounded for our transgressions, he was bruised for our iniquities; the chastisement of our peace was upon him; and with his stripes we are healed. He was led as a lamb to the slaughter, and numbered with the transgressors; and condemned by Pontius Pilate as a malefactor, though he had first declared Him innocent. Therefore, He restored that which he took not away, and suffered, the righteous for the unrighteous, as well in His body as in His soul, feeling the terrible punishment which our sins had merited; insomuch that his sweat became as it were great drops of blood falling down upon the ground. He called out: My God, my God, why hast thou forsaken me? and has suffered all this for the remission of our sins.

Wherefore we justly say with the apostle Paul that we know nothing save Jesus Christ, and him crucified; we count all things but loss and refuse for the excellency of the knowledge of Christ Jesus our Lord, in whose wounds we find all manner of consolation. Neither is it necessary to seek or invent any other means of being reconciled to God than this only sacrifice, once offered, by which he hath perfected forever them that are sanctified. This is also the reason why He was called by the angel of God, JESUS, that is to say, SAVIOR, because He would save his people from their sins.

Article XXII

Our Justification Through Faith in Jesus Christ

We believe that, to attain the true knowledge of this great mystery, the Holy Spirit kindles in our hearts an upright faith, which embraces Jesus Christ with all His merits, appropriates Him, and seeks nothing more besides Him. For it must needs follow, either that all things which are requisite to our salvation are not in Jesus Christ, or if all things are in Him, that then those who possess Jesus Christ through faith have complete salvation in Him. Therefore, for any to assert that Christ is not sufficient, but that something more is required besides Him, would be too gross a blasphemy; for hence it would follow that Christ was but half a Savior.

Therefore we justly say with Paul, that we are justified by faith alone, or by faith apart from works. However, to speak more clearly, we do not mean that faith itself justifies us, for it is only an instrument with which we embrace Christ our righteousness. But Jesus Christ, imputing to us all His merits, and so many holy works which He has done for us and in our stead, is our righteousness. And faith is an instrument that keeps us in communion with Him in all His benefits, which, when they become ours, are more than sufficient to acquit us of our sins.

Article XXIII

Wherein Our Justification Before God Consists

We believe that our salvation consists in the remission of our sins for Jesus Christ's sake, and that therein our righteousness before God is implied; as David and Paul teach us, declaring this to be the blessedness of man that God imputes righteousness to him apart from works. And the same apostle says that we are justified freely by his grace, through the redemption that is in Christ Jesus.

And therefore we always hold fast this foundation, ascribing all the glory to God, humbling ourselves before Him, and acknowledging ourselves to be such as we really are, without presuming to trust in anything in ourselves, or in any merit of ours, relying and resting upon the obedience of Christ crucified alone, which becomes ours when we believe in Him. This is sufficient to cover all our iniquities, and to give us confidence in approaching to God; freeing the conscience of fear, terror, and dread, without following the example of our first father, Adam, who, trembling, attempted to cover himself with fig-leaves. And, verily, if we should appear before God, relying on ourselves or on any other creature, though ever so little, we should, alas! be consumed. And therefore every one must pray with David: O Jehovah, enter not into judgment with thy servant: for in thy sight no man living is righteous.

Article XXIV

Mans Sanctification and Good Works

We believe that this true faith, being wrought in man by the hearing of the Word of God and the operation of the Holy Spirit, sanctifies him and makes him a new man, causing him to live a new life, and freeing him from the bondage of sin. Therefore it is so far from being true that this justifying faith makes men remiss in a pious and holy life, that on the contrary without it they would never do anything out of love to

God, but only out of self-love or fear of damnation. Therefore it is impossible that this holy faith can be unfruitful in man; for we do not speak of a vain faith, but of such a faith which is called in Scripture a faith working through love, which excites man to the practice of those works which God has commanded in His Word.

These works, as they proceed from the good root of faith, are good and acceptable in the sight of God, forasmuch as they are all sanctified by His grace. Nevertheless they are of no account towards our justification, for it is by faith in Christ that we are justified, even before we do good works; otherwise they could not be good works, any more than the fruit of a tree can be good before the tree itself is good.

Therefore we do good works, but not to merit by them (for what can we merit?); nay, we are indebted to God for the good works we do, and not He to us, since it is He who worketh in us both to will and to work, for his good pleasure. Let us therefore attend to what is written: When ye shall have done all the things that are commanded you, say, We are unprofitable servants; we have done that which it was our duty to do. In the meantime we do not deny that God rewards good works, but it is through His grace that He crowns His gifts.

Moreover, though we do good works, we do not found our salvation upon them; for we can do no work but what is polluted by our flesh, and also punishable; and although we could perform such works, still the remembrance of one sin is sufficient to make God reject them. Thus, then, we would always be in doubt, tossed to and fro without any certainty, and our poor consciences would be continually vexed if they relied not on the merits of the suffering and death of our Savior.

Article XXV

The Abolishing of the Ceremonial Law

We believe that the ceremonies and symbols of the law ceased at the coming of Christ, and that all the shadows are accomplished; so that the use of them must be abolished among Christians; yet the truth and substance of them remain with us in Jesus Christ, in whom they have their completion. In the meantime we still use the testimonies taken out of the law and the prophets to confirm us in the doctrine of the

115

gospel, and to regulate our life in all honorableness to the glory of God, according to His will.

Article XXVI

Christ's Intercession

We believe that we have no access unto God but alone through the only Mediator and Advocate, Jesus Christ the righteous; who therefore became man, having united in one person the divine and human natures, that we men might have access to the divine Majesty, which access would otherwise be barred against us. But this Mediator, whom the Father has appointed between Him and us, ought in no wise to affright us by His majesty, or cause us to seek another according to our fancy. For there is no creature, either in heaven or on earth, who loves us more than Jesus Christ; who, though existing in the form of God, yet emptied himself, being made in the likeness of men and of a servant for us, and in all things was made like unto his brethren. If, then, we should seek for another mediator who would be favorably inclined towards us, whom could we find who loved us more than He who laid down His life for us, even while we were his enemies? And if we seek for one who has power and majesty, who is there that has so much of both as He who sits at the right hand of God and to whom hath been given all authority in heaven and on earth? And who will sooner be heard than the own well beloved Son of God?

Therefore it was only through distrust that this practice of dishonoring, instead of honoring, the saints was introduced, doing that which they never have done nor required, but have on the contrary steadfastly rejected according to their bounden duty, as appears by their writings. Neither must we plead here our unworthiness; for the meaning is not that we should offer our prayers to God on the ground of our own worthiness, but only on the ground of the excellency and worthiness of the Lord Jesus Christ, whose righteousness is become ours by faith.

Therefore the apostle, to remove this foolish fear, or rather distrust, from us, rightly says that Jesus Christ in all things was made like unto his brethren, that he might become a merciful and faithful high priest, to make propitiation for the sins of the people. For in that he himself hath suffered being tempted, he is able to succor them that are tempted. And further to encourage us to go to Him, he says: Having then a great high priest, who hath passed through the heavens, Jesus the Son of God, let us hold fast our confession. For we have not a high priest that cannot be touched with the feeling of our infirmities; but one that hath been in all points tempted like aswe are, yet without sin. Let us therefore draw near with boldness unto the throne of grace, that we may receive mercy, and may find grace to help us in time of need. The same apostle says: Having boldness to enter into the holy place by the blood of Jesus, let us draw near with a true heart in fullness of faith, etc. Likewise: Christ hath his priesthood unchangeable; wherefore also he is able to save to the uttermost them that draw near unto God through him, seeing he ever liveth to make intercession for them.

What more can be required? since Christ Himself says: I am the way, and the truth, and the life: no one cometh unto the Father, but by me. To what purpose should we, then, seek another advocate, since it has pleased God to give us His own Son as an Advocate? Let us not forsake Him to take another, or rather to seek after another, without ever being able to find him; for God well knew, when He gave Him to us, that we were sinners.

Therefore, according to the command of Christ, we call upon the heavenly Father through Jesus Christ our only Mediator, as we are taught in the Lords Prayer; being assured that whatever we ask of the Father in His Name will be granted us.

Article XXVII

The Catholic Christian Church

We believe and profess one catholic or universal Church, which is a holy congregation of true Christian believers, all expecting their salvation in Jesus Christ, being washed by His blood, sanctified and sealed by the Holy Spirit.

This Church has been from the beginning of the world, and will be to the end thereof; which is evident from this that Christ is an eternal King, which without subjects He cannot be. And this holy Church is preserved or supported by God against the rage of the whole world; though it sometimes for a while appears very small, and in the eyes of men to be reduced to nothing; as during the perilous reign of Ahab the Lord reserved unto Him seven thousand men who had not bowed their knees to Baal.

Furthermore, this holy Church is not confined, bound, or limited to a certain place or to certain persons, but is spread and dispersed over the whole world; and yet is joined and united with heart and will, by the power of faith, in one and the same Spirit.

Article XXVIII

Every One Is Bound to Join Himself to the True Church

We believe, since this holy congregation is an assembly of those who are saved, and outside of it there is no salvation, that no person of whatsoever state or condition he may be, ought to withdraw from it, content to be by himself; but that all men are in duty bound to join and unite themselves with it; maintaining the unity of the Church; submitting themselves to the doctrine and discipline thereof; bowing their necks under the yoke of Jesus Christ; and as mutual members of the same body, serving to the edification of the brethren, according to the talents God has given them.

And that this may be the more effectually observed, it is the duty of all believers, according to the Word of God, to separate themselves from all those who do not belong to the Church, and to join themselves to this congregation, wheresoever God has established it, even though the magistrates and edicts of princes were against it, yea, though they should suffer death or any other corporal punishment. Therefore all those who separate themselves from the same or do not join themselves to it act contrary to the ordinance of God.

Article XXIX

The Marks of the True Church, and Wherein it Differs from the False Church

We believe that we ought diligently and circumspectly to discern from the Word of God which is the true Church, since all sects which are in the world assume to themselves the name of the Church. But we speak not here of hypocrites, who are mixed in the Church with the good, yet are not of the Church, though externally in it; but we say that the body and communion of the true Church must be distinguished from all sects that call themselves the Church.

The marks by which the true Church is known are these: If the pure doctrine of the gospel is preached therein; if it maintains the pure administration of the sacraments as instituted by Christ; if church discipline is exercised in chastening of sin; in short, if all things are managed according to the pure Word of God, all things contrary thereto rejected, and Jesus Christ acknowledged as the only Head of the Church. Hereby the true Church may certainly be known, from which no man has a right to separate himself.

With respect to those who are members of the Church, they may be known by the marks of Christians; namely, by faith, and when, having received Jesus Christ the only Savior, they avoid sin, follow after righteousness, love the true God and their neighbor, neither turn aside to the right or left, and crucify the flesh with the works thereof. But this is not to be understood as if there did not remain in them great infirmities; but they fight against them through the Spirit all the days of their life, continually taking their refuge in the blood, death, passion, and obedience of our Lord Jesus Christ, in whom they have remission of sins, through faith in Him.

As for the false Church, it ascribes more power and authority to itself and its ordinances than to the Word of God, and will not submit itself to the yoke of Christ. Neither does it administer the sacra ments as appointed by Christ in His Word, but adds to and takes from them, as it thinks proper; it relies more upon men than upon Christ; and persecutes those who live holily according to the Word of God and rebuke it for its errors, covetousness, and idolatry.

These two Churches are easily known and distinguished from each other.

Article XXX

The Government of the Church and its Offices

We believe that this true Church must be governed by that spiritual polity which our Lord has taught us in His Word; namely, that there must be ministers or pastors to preach the Word of God and to administer the sacraments; also elders and deacons, who, together with the pastors, form the council of the Church; that by these means the true religion may be preserved, and the true doctrine everywhere propagated, likewise transgressors chastened and restrained by spiritual means; also that the poor and distressed may be relieved and comforted, according to their necessities. By these means everything will be carried on in the Church with good order and decency, when faithful men are chosen, according to the rule prescribed by St. Paul in his Epistle to Timothy.

Article XXXI

The Ministers, Elders, and Deacons

We believe that the ministers of Gods Word, the elders, and the deacons ought to be chosen to their respective offices by a lawful election by the Church, with calling upon the name of the Lord, and in that order which the Word of God teaches. Therefore every one must take heed not to intrude himself by improper means, but is bound to wait till it shall please God to call him; that he may have testimony of his calling, and be certain and assured that it is of the Lord.

As for the ministers of Gods Word, they have equally the same power and authority wheresoever they are, as they are all ministers of Christ, the only universal Bishop and the only Head of the Church.

Moreover, in order that this holy ordinance of God may not be violated or slighted, we say that every one ought to esteem the ministers of Gods Word and the elders of the Church very highly for their works sake, and be at peace with them without murmuring, strife, or contention, as much as possible.

Article XXXII

The Order and Discipline of the Church

In the meantime we believe, though it is useful and beneficial that those who are rulers of the Church institute and establish certain ordinances among themselves for maintaining the body of the Church, yet that they ought studiously to take care that they do not depart from those things which Christ, our only Master, has instituted. And therefore we reject all human inventions, and all laws which man would introduce into the worship of God, thereby to bind and compel the conscience in any manner whatever. Therefore we admit only of that which tends to nourish and preserve concord and unity, and to keep all men in obedience to God. For this purpose, excommunication or church discipline is requisite, with all that pertains to it, according to the Word of God.

Article XXXIII

The Sacraments

We believe that our gracious God, taking account of our weakness and infirmities, has ordained the sacraments for us, thereby to seal unto us His promises, and to be pledges of the good will and grace of God towards us, and also to nourish and strengthen our faith; which He has joined to the Word of the gospel, the better to present to our senses both that which He declares to us by His Word and that which He works inwardly in our hearts, thereby confirming in us the salvation which He imparts to us. For they are visible signs and seals of an inward and invisible thing, by means whereof God works in us by the power of the Holy Spirit. Therefore the signs are not empty or meaningless, so as to deceive us. For Jesus Christ is the true object presented by them, without whom they would be of no moment.

Moreover, we are satisfied with the number of sacraments which Christ our Lord has instituted, which are two only, namely, the sacrament of baptism and the holy supper of our Lord Jesus Christ.

Article XXXIV

Holy Baptism

We believe and confess that Jesus Christ, who is the end of the law, has made an end, by the shedding of His blood, of all other sheddings of blood which men could or would make as a propitiation or satisfaction for sin; and that He, having abolished circumcision, which was done with blood, has instituted the sacrament of baptism instead thereof; by which we are received into the Church of God, and separated from all other people and strange religions, that we may wholly belong to Him whose mark and ensign we bear; and which serves as a testimony to us that He will forever be our gracious God and Father.

Therefore He has commanded all those who are His to be baptized with pure water, into the name of the Father and of the Son and of the Holy Spirit , thereby signifying to us, that as water washes away the filth of the body when poured upon it, and is seen on the body of the baptized when sprinkled upon him, so does the blood of Christ by the power of the Holy Spirit internally sprinkle the soul, cleanse it from its sins, and regenerate us from children of wrath unto children of God. Not that this is effected by the external water, but by the sprinkling of the precious blood of the Son of God; who is our Red Sea, through which we must pass to escape the tyranny of Pharaoh, that is, the devil, and to enter into the spiritual land of Canaan.

The ministers, therefore, on their part administer the sacrament and that which is visible, but our Lord gives that which is signified by the sacrament, namely, the gifts and invisible grace; washing, cleansing, and purging our souls of all filth and unrighteousness; renewing our hearts and filling them with all comfort; giving unto us a true assurance of His fatherly goodness; putting on us the new man, and putting off the old man with all his deeds.

We believe, therefore, that every man who is earnestly studious of obtaining life eternal ought to be baptized but once with this only baptism, without ever repeating the same, since we cannot be born twice. Neither does this baptism avail us only at the time when the water is poured upon us and received by us, but also through the whole course of our life.

Therefore we detest the error of the Anabaptists, who are not content with the one only baptism they have once received, and moreover condemn the baptism of the infants of believers, who we believe ought to be baptized and sealed with the sign of the covenant, as the children in Israel formerly were circumcised upon the same promises which are made unto our children. And indeed Christ shed His blood no less for the washing of the children of believers than for adult persons; and therefore they ought to receive the sign and sacrament of that which Christ has done for them; as the Lord commanded in the law that they should be made partakers of the sacrament of Christ's suffering and death shortly after they were born, by offering for them a lamb, which was a sacrament of Jesus Christ. Moreover, what circumcision was to the Jews, baptism is to our children. And for this reason St. Paul calls baptism the circumcision of Christ.

Article XXXV

The Holy Supper of Our Lord Jesus Christ

We believe and confess that our Savior Jesus Christ did ordain and institute the sacrament of the holy supper to nourish and support those whom He has already regenerated and incorporated into His family, which is His Church.

Now those who are regenerated have in them a twofold life, the one corporal and temporal, which they have from the first birth and is common to all men; the other, spiritual and heavenly, which is given them in their second birth, which is effected by the Word of the gospel, in the communion of the body of Christ; and this life is not common, but is peculiar to Gods elect. In like manner God has given us, for the support of the bodily and earthly life, earthly and common bread, which is subservient thereto and is common to all men, even as life itself. But for the support of the spiritual and heavenly life which believers have He has sent a living bread, which descended from heaven, namely, Jesus Christ, who nourishes and strengthens the spiritual life of believers when they eat Him, that is to say, when they appropriate and receive Him by faith in the spirit.

In order that He might represent unto us this spiritual and heavenly bread, Christ has instituted an earthly and visible bread as a sacrament of His body, and wine as a sacrament of His blood, to testify by them unto us that, as certainly as we receive and hold this sacrament in our hands and eat and drink the same with our mouths, by which our life is afterwards nourished, we also do as certainly receive by faith (which is the hand and mouth of our soul) the true body and blood of Christ our only Savior in our souls, for the support of our spiritual life.

Now, as it is certain and beyond all doubt that Jesus Christ has not enjoined to us the use of His sacraments in vain, so He works in us all that He represents to us by these holy signs, though the manner surpasses our understanding and cannot be comprehended by us, as the operations of the Holy Spirit are hidden and incomprehensible. In the meantime we err not when we say that what is eaten and drunk by us is the proper and natural body and the proper blood of Christ. But the manner of our partaking of the same is not by the mouth, but by the spirit through faith. Thus, then, though Christ always sits at the right hand of His Father in the heavens, yet does He not therefore cease to make us partakers of Himself by faith. This feast is a spiritual table, at which Christ communicates Himself with all His benefits to us, and gives us there to enjoy both Himself and the merits of His sufferings and death: nourishing, strengthening, and comforting our poor comfortless souls by the eating of His flesh, quickening and refreshing them by the drinking of His blood.

Further, though the sacraments are connected with the thing signified nevertheless both are not received by all men. The ungodly indeed receives the sacrament to his condemnation, but he does not receive the truth of the sacrament, even as Judas and Simon the sorcerer both indeed received the sacrament but not Christ who was signified by it, of whom believers only are made partakers.

Lastly, we receive this holy sacrament in the assembly of the people of God, with humility and reverence, keeping up among us a holy remembrance of the death of Christ our Savior, with thanksgiving, making there confession of our faith and of the Christian religion. Therefore no one ought to come to this table without having previously rightly examined himself, lest by eating of this bread and drinking of this cup he eat and drink judgment to himself. In a word, we are moved by the use of this holy sacrament to a fervent love towards God and our neighbor.

Therefore we reject all mixtures and damnable inventions which men have added unto and blended with the sacraments, as profanations of them; and affirm that we ought to rest satisfied with the ordinance which Christ and His apostles have taught us, and that we must speak of them in the same manner as they have spoken.

Article XXXVI

The Magistracy (Civil Government)

We believe that our gracious God, because of the depravity of mankind, has appointed kings, princes, and magistrates; willing that the world should be governed by certain laws and policies; to the end that the dissoluteness of men might be restrained, and all things carried on among them with good order and decency. For this purpose He has invested the magistracy with the sword for the punishment of evildoers and for the protection of them that do well .

Their office is not only to have regard unto and watch for the welfare of the civil state, but also to protect the sacred ministry, that the kingdom of Christ may thus be promoted. They must therefore countenance the preaching of the Word of the gospel everywhere, that God may be honored and worshipped by every one, as He commands in His Word.

Moreover, it is the bounden duty of every one, of whatever state, quality, or condition he may be, to subject himself to the magistrates; to pay tribute, to show due honor and respect to them, and to obey them in all things which are not repugnant to the Word of God; to supplicate for them in their prayers that God may rule and guide them in all their ways, and that we may lead a tranquil and quiet life in all godliness and gravity.

Wherefore we detest the Anabaptists and other seditious people, and in general all those who reject the higher powers and magistrates and would subvert justice, introduce community of goods, and confound that decency and good order which God has established among men.

Article XXXVII

The Last Judgment

Finally, we believe, according to the Word of God, when the time appointed by the Lord (which is unknown to all creatures) is come and the number of the elect complete, that our Lord Jesus Christ will come from heaven, corporally and visibly, as He ascended, with great glory and majesty to declare Himself Judge of the living and the dead, burning this old world with fire and flame to cleanse it.

Then all men will personally appear before this great Judge, both men and women and children, that have been from the beginning of the world to the end thereof, being summoned by the voice of the archangel, and by the sound of the trump of God. For all the dead shall be raised out of the earth, and their souls joined and united with their proper bodies in which they formerly lived. As for those who shall then be living, they shall not die as the others, but be changed in the twinkling of an eye, and from corruptible become incorruptible. Then the books shall be opened, and the dead judged according to what they shall have done in this world, whether it be good or evil. Nay, all men shall give account of every idle word they have spoken , which the world only counts amusement and jest; and then the secrets and hypocrisy of men shall be disclosed and laid open before all.

And therefore the consideration of this judgment is justly terrible and dreadful to the wicked and ungodly, but most desirable and comfortable to the righteous and elect; because then their full deliver ance shall be perfected, and there they shall receive the fruits of their labor and trouble which they have borne. Their innocence shall be known to all, and they shall see the terrible vengeance which God shall execute on the wicked, who most cruelly persecuted, oppressed, and tormented them in this world, and who shall be convicted by the testimony of their own consciences, and shall become immortal, but only to be tormented in the eternal fire which is prepared for the devil and his angels.

But on the contrary, the faithful and elect shall be crowned with glory and honor; and the Son of God will confess their names before God His Father and His elect angels; all tears shall be wiped from their eyes; and their cause which is now condemned by many judges and magistrates as heretical and impious will then be known to be the cause of the Son of God. And for a gracious reward, the Lord will cause them to possess such a glory as never entered into the heart of man to conceive.

Therefore we expect that great day with a most ardent desire, to the end that we may fully enjoy the promises of God in Christ Jesus our Lord. AMEN. Amen, come, Lord Jesus. Rev. 22:20 .

Theological Declaration of Barmen

May 1934

An appeal to the Evangelical congregations and Christians in Germany

The Confessional Synod of the German Evangelical Church met in Barmen, May 29-31 1934. Here representatives from all the German confessional churches met with one accord in a confession of the one Lord of the one, holy, apostolic church.

In fidelity to their confession of faith, members of Lutheran, Reformed, and United churches sought a common message for the need and temptation of the church in our day. With gratitude to God they are convinced that they have been given a common word to utter.

It was not their intention to found a new church or to form a union. For nothing was farther from their minds than the abolition of the confessional status of our churches. Their intention was, rather, to withstand in faith and unanimity the destruction of the confession of faith, and thus of the Evangelical Church in Germany.

In opposition to attempts to establish the unity of the German Evangelical Church by means of false doctrine, by the use of force and by insincere practices, the Confessional Synod insists that the unity of the Evangelical Churches in Germany can come only from the Word of God in faith through the Holy Spirit. Thus alone is the church renewed.

Therefore the Confessional Synod calls upon the congregations to range themselves behind it in prayer, and steadfastly to gather around those pastors and teachers who are loyal to the confessions.

Be not deceived by loose talk, as if we meant to oppose the unity of the German nation! Do not listen to the seducers who pervert our intentions, as if we wanted to break up the unity of the German Evangelical Church or to forsake the confessions of the Fathers!

Try the spirits whether they are of God! Prove also the words of the Confessional Synod of the German Evangelical Church to see whether they agree with holy scripture and with the confessions of the Fathers.

If you find that we are speaking contrary to scripture, then do not listen to us! But if you find that we are taking our stand upon scripture, then let no fear or temptation keep you from treading with us the path of faith and obedience to the Word of God, in order that God's people be of one mind upon earth and that we in faith experience what he himself has said: "I will never leave you, nor forsake you." Therefore, "Fear not, little flock, for it is your Father's good pleasure to give you the kingdom."

Theological declaration concerning the present situation of the German Evangelical Church

According to the opening words of its constitution of July 11 1933, the German Evangelical Church is a federation of confessional churches that grew our of the Reformation and that enjoy equal rights. The theological basis for the unification of these churches is laid down in Article 1 and Article 2 (1) of the constitution of the German Evangelical Church that was recognized by the Reich government on July 14 1933:

- Article 1. The inviolable foundation of the German Evangelical Church is the gospel of Jesus Christ as it is attested for us in holy scripture and brought to light again in the confessions of the Reformation. The full powers that the church needs for its mission are hereby determined and limited.
- Article 2 (1). The German Evangelical Church is divided into member churches (Landeskirchen).

We, the representatives of Lutheran, Reformed, and United churches, of free synods, church assemblies, and parish organizations united in the Confessional Synod of the German Evangelical Church, declare that we stand together on the ground of the German Evangelical Church as a federation of German confessional churches. We are bound together by the confession of the one Lord of the one, holy, catholic, and apostolic church.

We publicly declare before all evangelical churches in Germany that what they hold in common in this confession is grievously imperilled, and with it the unity of the German Evangelical Church. It is threatened by the teaching methods and actions of the ruling church party of the "German Christians" and of the church administration carried on by them. These have become more and more apparent during the first year of the existence of the German Evangelical Church. This threat consists in the fact that the theological basis on which the German Evangelical Church is united has been continually and systematically thwarted and rendered ineffective by alien principles, on the part of the leaders and spokesmen of the "German Christians" as well as on the part of the church administration. When these principles are held to be valid, then, according to all the confessions in force among us, the church ceases to be the church and the German Evangelical Church, as a federation of confessional churches, becomes intrinsically impossible.

As members of Lutheran, Reformed, and United churches we may and must speak with one voice in this matter today. Precisely because we want to be and to remain faithful to our various confessions, we may not keep silent, since we believe that we have been given a common message to utter in a time of common need and temptation. We commend to God what this may mean for the interrelations of the confessional churches.

In view of the errors of the "German Christians" of the present Reich church government which are devastating the church and also therefore breaking up the unity of the German Evangelical Church, we confess the following evangelical truths:

1. "I am the way, and the truth, and the life; no one comes to the Father, but by me." (Jn 14.6) "Truly, truly, I say to you, he who does not enter the sheepfold by the door, but climbs in by another way, that man is a thief and a robber... I am the door; if anyone enters by me, he will be saved." (Jn 10.1, 9)

Jesus Christ, as he is attested for us in holy scripture, is the one Word of God which we have to hear and which we have to trust and obey in life and in death.

We reject the false doctrine, as though the church could and would have to acknowledge as a source of its proclamation, apart from and besides this one Word of God, still other events and powers, figures and truths, as God's revelation.

2. "Christ Jesus, whom God has made our wisdom, our righteousness and sanctification and redemption." (1 Cor 1.30)

As Jesus Christ is God's assurance of the forgiveness of all our sins, so, in the same way and with the same seriousness he is also God's mighty claim upon our whole life. Through him befalls us a joyful deliverance from the godless fetters of this world for a free, grateful service to his creatures.

We reject the false doctrine, as though there were areas of our life in which we would not belong to Jesus Christ, but to other lords - areas in which we would not need justification and sanctification through him.

3. "Rather, speaking the truth in love, we are to grow up in every way into him who is the head, into Christ, from whom the whole body [is] joined and knit together." (Eph 4.15,16)

The Christian church is the congregation of the brethren in which Jesus Christ acts presently as the Lord in word and sacrament through the Holy Spirit. As the church of pardoned sinners, it has to testify in the midst of a sinful world, with its faith as with its obedience, with its message as with its order, that it is solely his property, and that it lives and wants to live solely from his comfort and from his direction in the expectation of his appearance.

We reject the false doctrine, as though the church were permitted to abandon the form of its message and order to its own pleasure or to changes in prevailing ideological and political convictions.

4. "You know that the rulers of the gentiles lord it over them, and their great men exercise authority over them. It shall not be so among you;

but whoever would be great among you must be your servant." (Mt 20.25,26)

The various offices in the church do not establish a dominion of some over the others; on the contrary, they are for the exercise of the ministry entrusted to and enjoined upon the whole congregation.

We reject the false doctrine, as though the church, apart from this ministry, could and were permitted to give itself, or allow to be given to it, special leaders vested with ruling powers.

5. "Fear God. Honour the emperor." (1 Pet 2.17)

Scripture tells us that, in the as yet unredeemed world in which the church also exists, the state has by divine appointment the task of providing for justice and peace. [It fulfils this task] by means of the threat and exercise of force, according to the measure of human judgment and human ability. The church acknowledges the benefit of this divine appointment in gratitude and reverence before him. It calls to mind the kingdom of God, God's commandment and righteousness, and thereby the responsibility both of rulers and of the ruled. It trusts and obeys the power of the Word by which God upholds all things.

We reject the false doctrine, as though the state, over and beyond its special commission, should and could become the single and totalitarian order of human life, thus fulfilling the church's vocation as well.

We reject the false doctrine, as though the church, over and beyond its special commission, should and could appropriate the characteristics, the tasks, and the dignity of the state, thus itself becoming an organ of the state.

6. "Lo, I am with you always, to the close of the age." (Mt 28.20) "The word of God is not fettered." (2 Tim 2.9)

The church's commission, upon which its freedom is founded, consists in delivering the message of the free grace of God to all people in Christ's stead, and therefore in the ministry of his own Word and work through sermon and sacrament.

We reject the false doctrine, as though the church in human arrogance could place the word and work of the Lord in the service of any arbitrarily chosen desires, purposes, and plans.

The Confessional Synod of the German Evangelical Church declares that it sees in the acknowledgement of these truths and in the rejection of these errors the indispensable theological basis of the German Evangelical Church as a federation of confessional churches. It invites all who are able to accept its declaration to be mindful of these theological principles in their decisions in church politics. It entreats all whom it concerns to return to the unity of faith, love, and hope.

Also from Benediction Books ...

Wandering Between Two Worlds: Essays on Faith and Art
Anita Mathias
Benediction Books, 2007
152 pages
ISBN: 0955373700

Available from www.amazon.com, www.amazon.co.uk
www.wanderingbetweentwoworlds.com

In these wide-ranging lyrical essays, Anita Mathias writes, in lush, lovely prose, of her naughty Catholic childhood in Jamshedpur, India; her large, eccentric family in Mangalore, a sea-coast town converted by the Portuguese in the sixteenth century; her rebellion and atheism as a teenager in her Himalayan boarding school, run by German missionary nuns, St. Mary's Convent, Nainital; and her abrupt religious conversion after which she entered Mother Teresa's convent in Calcutta as a novice. Later rich, elegant essays explore the dualities of her life as a writer, mother, and Christian in the United States-- Domesticity and Art, Writing and Prayer, and the experience of being "an alien and stranger" as an immigrant in America, sensing the need for roots.

About the Author

Anita Mathias was born in India, has a B.A. and M.A. in English from Somerville College, Oxford University and an M.A. in Creative Writing from the Ohio State University. Her essays have been published in The Washington Post, The London Magazine, The Virginia Quarterly Review, Commonweal, Notre Dame Magazine, America, The Christian Century, Religion Online, The Southwest Review, Contemporary Literary Criticism, New Letters, The Journal, and two of HarperSanFrancisco's The Best Spiritual Writing anthologies. Her non-fiction has won fellowships from The National Endowment for the Arts; The Minnesota State Arts Board; The Jerome Foundation, The Vermont Studio Center; The Virginia Centre for the Creative Arts, and the First Prize for the Best General Interest Article from the Catholic Press Association of the United States and Canada. Anita has taught Creative Writing at the College of William and Mary, and now lives and writes in Oxford, England.

CPSIA information can be obtained at www.ICGtesting.com
Printed in the USA
LVOW041529041012

301525LV00004B/82/P